The Book of

Destiny

Your Questions Answered

The Book of
Destiny

Your Questions Answered

Barbara Meiklejohn-Free

Flavia Kate Peters

MOON
BOOKS

Winchester, UK
Washington, USA

First published by Moon Books, 2015
Moon Books is an imprint of John Hunt Publishing Ltd., Laurel House, Station Approach,
Alresford, Hants, SO24 9JH, UK
office1@jhpbooks.net
www.johnhuntpublishing.com
www.moon-books.net

For distributor details and how to order please visit the 'Ordering' section on our website.

Text copyright: Barbara Meiklejohn-Free and Flavia Kate Peters 2014

ISBN: 978 1 78279 945 0
Library of Congress Control Number: 2014958359

A CIP catalogue record for this book is available from the British Library.

Design: Stuart Davies
www.stuartdaviesart.com

Printed and bound by CPI Group (UK) Ltd, Croydon, CR0 4YY

We operate a distinctive and ethical publishing philosophy in all
areas of our business, from our global network of authors to
production and worldwide distribution.

Dedications

To all the unknown wise men and women who gifted to us
with old sayings that we still use today.

To the prophets, sages, oracles and seers of the ancients who
shared their many visions, their guidance and their wisdom.

Thank you

Introduction

Imagine yourself in an old dusty attic room. It is filled with relics from a forgotten time and as you look around you notice a worn trunk in the corner. You kneel before it and slowly lift its creaking lid. Searching through the contents, you find a large leather-bound book. Unable to determine the title, you carefully lift it up, blowing away the cobwebs and dust, till the words 'The Book of Destiny' appear. With trepidation you open the book...

You tentatively turn the pages, yellowed with age. You realise that this isn't any ordinary book, for it speaks to you of ancient secrets, words of the wise, and with a gasp you quickly shut it. For a moment you close your eyes, then taking a deep breath you open the book again. It falls to a page that appears to have been written especially for you. In that moment, the message tells you all you need to know. And you know in your heart that this is a book to treasure, to keep safe and revere. This is a book to open when you wish to draw upon the wisdom of Spirit. You are now the guardian, the keeper of The Book of Destiny and it is for your eyes only...

When Barbara shared with me her vision of *The Book of Destiny*, I knew that this was going to be something different, something special. Feelings of past lives started to well up inside of me and I saw great wisdom keepers of the ancients offering the people divine guidance and advice, as they shared their visions and insights. I connected with the essence of oracles of ancient lands, such as at Delphi, where large dusty books filled with esoteric secrets and sacred symbols were consulted before making decisions, giving advice or predicting the future. Sadly we can no longer visit these temples of the oracles, which is why Barbara and I have come together, along with Spirit of course, to share enlightening advice that is so often missing from our lives, in the form of this wonderful book.

1

The twist is that favourite old sayings are used as the titles for each message. When Barbara shared the sayings, collated over the years, memories surfaced from my past, especially from when I was a little girl. I remember being told, 'Be careful what you wish for,' without understanding why that could be a bad thing. It is only when we grow and learn from experience that the deeper meanings to these old and wise sayings of our ancestors make sense. I soon realised that many of these old sayings were still being used in conversations today – a marvel as I have found that some go way back to the times of old, such as the Middle Ages in England.

As I sat with each quote, preparing myself to write, I was surprised to find how the words of Spirit were easily accessed to perfectly complement each and every saying. The messages that came through me for each page offered perfect words of ancient wisdom to bring about practical assistance for this very modern world. This is a book of divination, a treasury of insights and the gift of very real messages from beloved Spirit to help, to motivate and advise. *The Book of Destiny* offers itself to you as your personal oracle. May you enjoy and grow from the many blessings that this is book designed to bring, as it accompanies you on your path and illuminates the way.

Brightest Blessings,
Flavia

Divining Your Destiny:
How to Use This Book

Words have power, so it is important that people are aware of what they are saying. I challenge you to listen to what you are saying, go out and find the origin and the true meaning of the words you have uttered. There is always a story behind a saying...

Welcome to *The Book of Destiny*. Here you will find insights into your life's purpose and desires. It will help you answer questions about love, money, work, relationships, health, the future and other issues.

Of all the wisdom practices I've experienced, what sticks most with me is the time I turned to Swain, my spiritual father and Highland Seer, for guidance about my mother's health. Without telling Swain why I had come, he said, *'I see a sunrise. Be prepared. Love.'* It was sunrise when my mother passed. Swain gifted me a picture, a saying of wisdom and a word of destiny. In that brief moment I understood all I needed to know. I experienced how a single conversation with a wise man could be better than ten years of study.

The inspiration for this book came whilst on the Big Island of Hawaii. The locals asked about some of the sayings I was using in my conversation, such as 'Better late than never.' That night in the dreamtime I was shown a vision of *The Book of Destiny* with pictures, sayings, key words and specific messages. When you feel ready to use this book make sure that you treat it with respect. The book is a divination tool and, like the tarot and decks of oracle cards, will attune to your energies and those of Spirit, to bring you the message that is right for you at the time. As you sit with the book, place your left hand on the front cover and your right hand on the back cover. You may to ask your spirit guides, ancestors or angels for help and guidance with the answer to your question, or ask the book itself. Take your time, and remember that you are seeking the wisdom of the oracle.

Once you have asked your question, focus your intention on 'true resolution' and with an open heart and mind open the book. You will feel guided to a certain page, or you may open it at random. Know that you cannot get it wrong. You will be greeted by an image, a word of 'destiny' the corresponding saying, a message and the word of destiny explanation. Take your time to look at the image. Does it make sense? If it does, keep the page open and reflect upon the image. What does it show you? What significance does the picture have to your present life at this present time?

Now take a look at the saying and the message that has presented itself to you. Reflect on these words. How can they be applied to your life and what you wish to achieve? Next focus on the destiny word, for this word has a meaning and a feeling behind it. What could this word mean for you? If the message does not seem to make sense, or you would like more information for your enquiry, then close the book and start again. You will be led to a new page that will back up the previous message and/or offer further insights. This book is also ideal if you wish to give readings and messages for others. You can use it in exactly the same way as you would for yourself. Ask the person to keep an open heart whilst asking the question. Open the book to reveal the answer... May your destiny be revealed in perfect divine order, as intended through these pages.

Blessed Be,
Barbara

1

'Crystal Clear'

Your judgements are being clouded at the moment by your expectations and fears, and those of others. You think you know what you want, but are unsure of how or what to ask for in order to bring it about. It's as though you can't see the wood for the trees. Taking time to focus on the subject of your enquiry is what you need to do right now, for clarity seeks you out and asks, 'What is it that you really want to know?' Getting back in touch with your true intuitive powers; listening with your heart and head requires bravery and honesty. You must be ready, and have regained your ability to discern between what is truly helpful for you and what a less authentic you might wish to hear or see. You are asked to be completely truthful with yourself as you gaze into the crystal ball. Here you will be shown the real question that in turn will give you the answer you are seeking.

Crystal Ball Revealed

Crystals have been used for thousands of years in many cultures for scrying and divination. The crystal ball acts as a focus for meditation and is a tool for clear sight and destiny foresight. Dr John Dee, occultist and adviser for Queen Elizabeth I (1527-1608), used a crystal ball for communication with the world of Spirit, on her behalf. **Crystal Ball reveals...** Be clear about your intentions. Work on expanding your third eye, in order to receive messages in the form of visions from Spirit. You need to be fully aware of a situation before making decisions. Communicate clearly to others in order to avoid misunderstandings.

Crystal Ball

Clarity

2

'Careful What You Wish For'

Your manifesting abilities are extremely powerful right now and what you desire can easily be made into form. Monitor your thoughts very carefully because what you are thinking about, and focussing on, is about to come true. Be aware of whether your thoughts are positive or negative, because this will manifest into your reality. Being aware of everything that flows through your mind and being conscientious is key to bringing about all that is good for you, and all others. What is it that you really want to draw into your life, and what would you rather not? This is a good time to drown any thoughts or words that do not serve you into the wishing well that has presented itself to you on this page. Now focus on all that you would like to come about, for the highest good. Be mindful as you throw your wishes, like coins, into the water in order for your dreams and aspirations to unfold and birth into your reality.

Wishing Well Revealed

Nordic myths talk of a well of wisdom called Mimir's well (Mímisbrunnr) that offered magical properties in exchange for the sacrifice of something held dear. The story expanded through European folklore and well-wishing became popular throughout. Coins were thrown into wells to appease the resident water spirits, in the hope that they would grant wishes in return. Traditions continue today at sacred wells all over the world. **Wishing Well reveals...** Make a list of all that you wish to bring into your life. Focus on the good, rather than fears and worries. Cleanse your energy field. Drink more water. Eat water-based foods such as fruit and salad.

Wishing Well

Conscientious

3

'Count Your Blessings'

Money is not the only way to fulfil your material and other needs. The universe is wonderful at meeting your requirements, and does so in many different ways, but not necessarily in the way you would expect. You may be gifted a book that has the knowledge you have been hoping for. A meal may be cooked for you, giving you the nourishment you require or a kind smile from a stranger may come your way when you need it the most. So look around you today and recognise all the signs and gifts that abound. The more you see and appreciate all that comes, the more you will receive. Do not limit yourself by believing that supplies will only come via money, this will block all that is waiting to come to you. Many people wish to win the lottery. But what they really desire is an abundance of money. The trouble here is that this request limits how the universe can deliver. It is important to ask for what you need and then be open to receive in all ways. The universe is waiting to do just that, and deliver to you right now. Know that this is a fortuitous moment, bringing about good luck and fortune

Numbers Revealed

Numbers are used in everyday life and are the language of the universe, as Pythagoras discovered. Numerology was used by the ancients and is a great source of divination and universal information. **Numbers reveals...** Return to studying. You are being helped from above with tests and exams. Do brain exercises to keep you alert. Make a list of all your blessings. Say gratitude prayers for all the good that is in your life.

Numbers

1 2 3
4 5 6
7
8 9

Fortuitous

4

'Time and Tide Wait for No Man'

The tides of change are afoot. You are being called to realise who you are and to be it – now! No longer must you procrastinate and put off until tomorrow what should have been done yesterday. Just do it! Time to shake off all doubts and fears for it is only the bold who are rewarded the realisation of their dreams and wishes. So if you do not recognise this tide of change you will miss the boat! Do not fear facing change, it is the natural cycle of life. Take a risk, to experience and be able to offer new strength and other gifts that are waiting for you as you follow the natural flow of what the universe is offering you. You are being urged to work with the natural cycles of the Moon as you open up your natural intuitive abilities. Let go of control and you will find it easier to move forward. Stop struggling against the tide, for it is time to sail into your destiny.

Moon Revealed

Babylonian astronomers and many other ancient cultures have revered and studied the effect of the cycles of the Moon. This sacred silver light is 4.5 billion years old and is actually a mirror to the Sun, lighting our way through the darkness of night. **Moon reveals...** You have past life knowledge of how to work with the Moon and its cycles. Join a Moon worship group. Make an altar dedicated to each Moon phase. Become aware of your own cycles and rhythms. You may be experiencing female gynaecological bodily changes. Go with the flow. Only do what feels naturally comfortable for you and recharge your batteries.

Moon

Mutable

5

'Your Past is Catching Up With You'

This message represents unfinished business. Within all relationships lie opportunities to resolve any issues, either in this life or from a previous lifetime, that you or both parties involved need to learn from. Someone from your past will soon turn up in order for you to fulfil lessons to be learned so that you, the other person, or both of you can move on from the present moment, either together or separately. The person who is coming back into your life may have been involved directly with this situation or as a catalyst which will help you with any resolutions. This is a very good omen as you are being offered the chance to reconcile any differences that have formed so that you may move on, taking with you peace and harmony into your future. At this time you are being asked to read between the lines. It is very important that instead of being ruled by judgement, as you can quite often be accused of doing, you should recognise the true blessing in this reunion.

Tea Leaves Revealed

Ancient Greeks, the Middle Eastern tribes and nomadic gypsies used this popular form of divination by reading people's fortunes from the leaves left in tea cups. Tea ceremonies still exist today in Japan as a Zen ritual that aims to remove the ego from the action. **Tea Leaves reveals...** Learn the ancient art of reading tea leaves. Investigate your ancestry to discover your gypsy blood. Make welcome that person you have avoided recently. Avoid drinking caffeine and switch to fruit or herbal teas.

Tea Leaves

Reunion

6

'A Bolt from the Blue'

You got it! This is your 'Aha' moment! You have been asking for something for a long time now and finally the answer and solution are about to hit you – just like that! Too often you have dismissed direct divine guidance, mistaking it for your own thoughts which you have then analysed and pushed to the back of your mind. It is time for you to realise your natural claircognizant (clear knowing) abilities and know that this is how you receive your messages from Spirit. Accepting your gift will enable you to clearly understand and recognise the next step required. The universe has been waiting for you to claim your talent and to embrace the guidance that you have so readily ignored. It is time to acknowledge your divinely inspired ideas and believe in yourself. Like a firework display, your ideas will be lit up like a beacon and sparks will really fly to make you finally sit up and take notice. This will illuminate your way as you follow and trust what guidance you have been given.

Lightning Revealed

Thunder and lightning bolts are thought to be divine weapons and symbols of the Gods' dominion over the elements. Zeus, the king of the Greek pantheon, and Thor, of Germanic mythology, are among the Gods who utilise lightning for removing obstacles and for regeneration. **Lightning reveals...** You will be receiving an idea that must not be ignored. The right pathway for you will be beckoning. Be the light and allow your soul to shine. An unexpected situation will arise – be ready to embrace it. See the good in all things and you shall receive abundantly.

Lightning

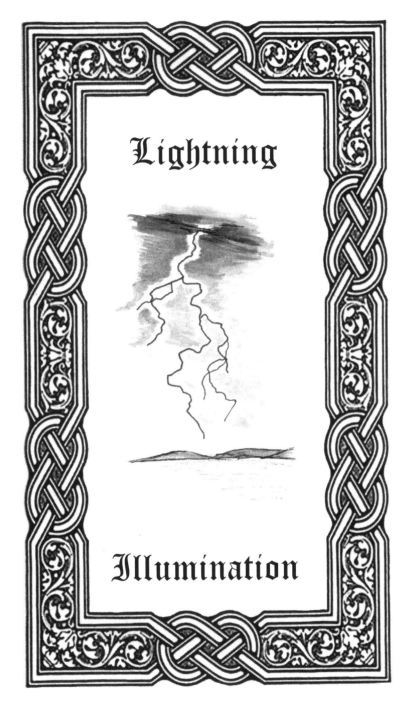

Illumination

7

'Better Late Than Never'

It is about time that you put yourself before others. When are you going to realise that you cannot heal the world until you are in fact healed first? For too long you have been concerned for others and have neglected your own needs. Stop! Take time to pamper yourself and have some 'me time'. For centuries it has been ingrained in us to put others first and ourselves last. This, sadly, is the opposite of how we and the world heals. Loving and nurturing ourselves first, before all others, enables us to stand in wholeness and balance, giving us the strength and ability to help others, without draining our own life-force energy. When we are healed and whole our world becomes the same, healed and whole. When this is understood then it is 'healing mastery'. An easy, but effective affirmation for you to say each day is: 'I am healed and whole. I am healed and whole. I am healed and whole.'

Earth Revealed

Herodotus realised that all known names for the Earth are feminine such as Kali Ma, Shakti, Gaia and Erda to name but a few. The tenet 'as above, so below' refers to the Sky being the father and the Earth the mother – the place of our birth, our home that feeds us, nurtures us, supports us and gives us all we need to survive. **Earth reveals...** Healing is important for you right now. Take time out to rest and nurture yourself. Remember to stay grounded. You are being called to be environmentally aware. Join an environmental group. Recycle and respect the natural world. Connect with and discover the healing benefits of the elemental kingdom.

Earth

Affirmation

8

'Swimming Against the Tide'

Stop trying to be the hero! This is one situation that you cannot save. You are using up energy on something that will never go the way you intend it to, no matter how hard you try. This is the one time you are being asked to back down and give it up – let go. As you stop trying to swim against the strong current you will find that instead of drowning, as you appear to be, life will become so much easier for you. Instead of struggling you will find that people, situations and what you desire will all flow to you naturally. From the moment you stop trying to control what you 'think' should be, then all will fall nicely into place. So, back off and just go with the flow and chill out. You will find that it is less effort and that you can use all that new and spare energy to invest in what you really enjoy. Allow it all to come to you and relax, for once in your life. For the moment you do, it will happen effortlessly. So stop the chattering of the mind, take a deep breath and just 'be'.

Salmon Revealed

The salmon was one of the most sacred creatures to the ancient Celts. The salmon teaches us that to gain wisdom and knowledge we have to return to our roots to spawn and regenerate from what we have learnt along the way. Salmon advocates rising above all the limitations that have been set in order to stop us from reaching our destiny. **Salmon reveals...** You have been struggling lately. If something doesn't feel right then trust your intuition. Stop and take stock of where your life is heading. Follow the direction that feels right for you. Take time out to pray and meditate. Rise above any problems and see the bigger picture.

Salmon

Heroic

9

'A Lucky Break'

Your patience has paid off and you are to be rewarded! It may have seemed that you have waited for an age to bring about your desires, and many would have given up by now. By not negating all that you wished for, you have made manifest a wonderful outcome. You kept going, never giving up – a fabulous feat not many can claim! What you have been waiting for is finally coming. This will happen in ways that you didn't dream were possible. So just relax, knowing that everything has been taken care of. Now is the time to be in a loving state of receiving. All that has been prepared for you behind the scenes, whilst you were thinking positively and expectantly, is to become a reality for you now. Don't try to second guess how this will happen, as it could block the speed at which it comes through. Instead be open to receiving with gratitude as your dreams come true. Congratulations!

Wishbone Revealed

The Etruscans believed that fowl were soothsayers. After sacrificing the sacred bird, the Etruscans laid its wishbone in the sunshine to dry. This tradition was handed down to the Romans who then passed it on to the British who still, to this day, enjoy pulling the wishbone of a cooked chicken in two as they make a wish. Whoever receives the biggest part of the bone has their wish granted. **Wishbone reveals...** You have been wishing too hard for something. Relax and allow the universe to deliver. Use daily affirmations to bring about good fortune. Say prayers and wishes for yourself and others. Think of yourself in positive ways.

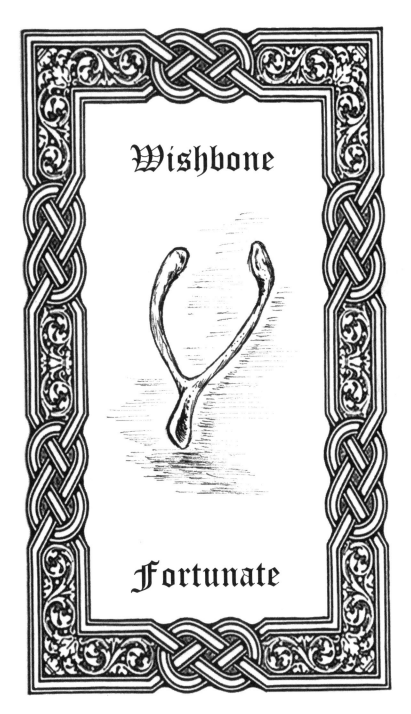

Wishbone

Fortunate

10

'Don't Turn a Blind Eye'

Open your eyes, time to wake up! Enough is enough. You have been stumbling through the darkness as though you have not wanted to see the light of truth that has tried to beam its way into your life. This is why this message has come to you now, to serve as a warning. There is a situation or a person in your life that does not serve your highest purpose. There is a lack of ethics here, even though they, or the situation, are being painted as righteous with rather saintly principles. All is not what it seems and deep down you actually know who, or what, this is but have chosen to ignore it. It may be all well and good wishing for harmony by not rocking the boat, but you must at least acknowledge the alarm bells that have been ringing within you. You know full well that this situation does not resonate with your own truth and integrity.

Eye Revealed

The eye is referred to as the window of the soul. In many cultures and traditions the eye represents the 'all-seeing eye' of protection and represents the 'God' within. **Eye reveals...** You are not allowing yourself to see the full truth. You like to see the good in everyone. You trust too easily. Investigate carefully before you make a decision. See yourself through another's eyes, in order to understand them. Do not be quick to make judgement. See only love within everyone. Look past any chaos to see perfect Divine order. Focus on opening your third eye chakra, to enable clear visions from Spirit. See the beauty within yourself and others.

Eye

Morality

11

'Learn to Walk, Before You Run'

Yes, you have an important life purpose. Yes, you are naturally gifted. Yes, all that you are asking for will be given. But all in good time! Everything in this universe has its natural order of things and that includes timing. You are so very keen to have everything now, for it all to happen immediately. You find it difficult that all you wish to be, all you wish to have, has not happened yet. This message has come upon the wings of a butterfly to assure you that these things will happen. But first you need to have patience. The butterfly is a beautiful creature, but has to go through various stages before it is able to reach its true potential. So allow everything to unfold naturally as it should do, keeping your eyes fixed firmly on the outcome, but enjoying every bit of the journey along the way.

Butterfly Revealed

Change and transformation are the key to the attributes of the butterfly. In ancient Greek the word for butterfly is 'psyche' which means 'soul'. The Celts believed that the butterfly was a human soul in search of a mother, and the Aztecs believed that a person's last breath was transformed into a butterfly. Butterflies awaken our spirits and open our hearts to our evolution and transformation. **Butterfly reveals...** It is time for the real you to emerge. Take steps towards freedom. Recognise that the struggle you are experiencing is for a greater outcome. Attract butterflies into your garden by planting buddleia. Let go of the old. New beginnings will bring many blessings.

Butterfly

Matamorphic

12

'Fight Fire with Fire'

Do not hold back! This is the time to scream and shout and let it all out! Okay, so you are all about the love and the light and that's beautiful, but this is not the time or the situation to be a wussy. Say it as it is, speak your truth and stand up (for once) and be counted. For too long now you have rolled over and played dead. You may seem to think that this is the proper way to behave, but it has, in fact, been restricting you and quashing your feelings. Which is why you are about to erupt! So go on, you will feel so much better after a rant and will find that afterwards you have found the equilibrium to handle subsequent situations. Working with the element of fire helps to ignite our strengths and inner power. Lighting a candle and staring into its flame will enable you to do just that. Breathe deeply in and out as you become aware of the spirits of the fire who will gently kindle that divine powerhouse within. As it expands and grows, so will your courage and vitality, thus enabling you to stand strong in your beliefs.

Volcano Revealed

Volcanoes were given a deity in the attempt to appease these fiery furnaces, including Vulcan, the Blacksmith God of the Romans and the Hawaiian Goddess Pele, who were revered by offerings and prayers by the people. **Volcano reveals...** This is a time of great transformation for you. Don't be afraid of your power. Take steps towards your desired career. Be honest with yourself. Follow your dreams. Re-ignite your passion for life and love. Recognise and use your strengths.

Volcano

Transform

13

'All that Glitters is not Gold'

Allow your inner vision to see through the illusion. Don't be dazzled by offers that seem too good to be true as appearances are deceptive. You are about to be made an offer that sounds as though your dreams could come true. They will do, but not through this vessel. Please don't be fooled by enticing words and promises as they will lure you into a world of false hope. You are being asked to step up and call upon your spiritual sight of clairvoyance (clear seeing) to enable you to see the whole picture. When you shine crystal clear light onto a situation, areas of darkness will be revealed. Do not be scared, but be relieved, for you have been saved from walking a path that would lead you from the light into the darkness. Instead be vigilant and use discernment as you allow and trust your intuition to be your true guide.

Crystal Skull Revealed

Found in the 1800s in Central and South America, including Mexico, these incredible crystals are cut and shaped against the axis, which continues to puzzle scientists to this day. Intriguing and mysterious these skulls are believed to hold ancient knowledge and wisdom to assist in awakening humans to a higher spiritual understanding. **Crystal Skull reveals...** You are receiving visions and greater esoteric understanding. Take a professional crystal healing course. Work with crystals in your everyday life. Your energy is being lifted to a higher vibration. Use your spiritual gifts for the service of others. Study alchemy. Keep your focus on the highest good.

Crystal
Skull

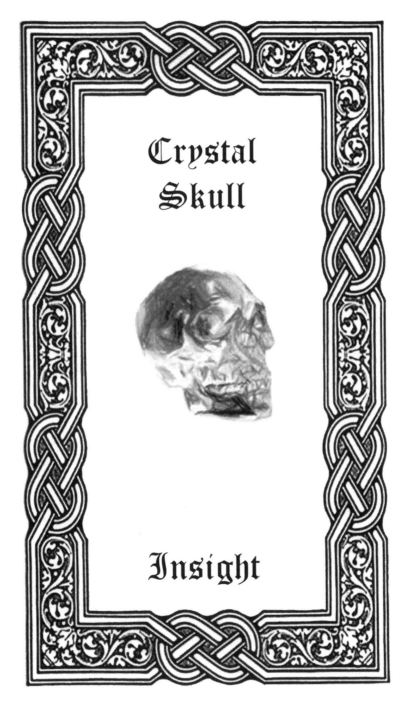

Insight

14

'Kiss and Make Up'

Let bygones be bygones. This is one relationship that you do want to save, and deep down you know that is exactly what you desire. Yes things were said that you didn't like. Deeds were done that you deemed unfair and have been playing out in your mind ever since. But please don't let things fester. If they do then it can only lead to bitterness and resentment. Over time these negative traits can manifest into great misery or even dis-ease – much better to swallow your pride and take the plunge towards reconciliation. Be brave, be bold and make the first move. You will be so pleased that you did, and through this action the outcome to returned peace and harmony is assured. The sacred mistletoe of the ancient Druids lends its energy to seal and seed your renewed friendship – one that will serve you well as you continue to walk the path of life together. Be strong and take the first step. Go on – you can do it!

Mistletoe Revealed

Sacred to the Druids and other Pagans, mistletoe is believed to hold healing powers, bringing good luck and blessings to every homestead. Today it is still traditional to kiss under the mistletoe and hang it over the doorway for protection. **Mistletoe reveals...** A wonderful romance is just around the corner. You have met your soul mate. A relationship is being healed. You are experiencing a power struggle. Let go of any defensiveness. Forgive and start again. This is a time for compassion and understanding. Make a list of all the things that you appreciate about your partner.

Mistletoe

Compatibility

15

'Are You of Right Mind?'

You are over-thinking things! Stop trying to analyse every conversation, every word, and every thought. You are driving yourself mad with this constant internal chatter, which is leading to self-chaos. So much so that you don't know what to think any more or which way you should go and it's all getting too much. Enough! It is time to shift from the control of your logical and analytical left brain. Instead you are being urged to shift into your creative, intuitive right brain, which has been lying dormant for too long now. Here you will find clarity, inspiration and the peace of mind that you seek in order to see things clearly so that you can take your next step without hesitation. Allow your inner vision to see through the illusion of fears. Instead focus on all that you would like to happen in your life. Remember that your mind can be your greatest enemy. Time to give your worries and concerns some time off, and welcome in some much needed peace and quiet

Head Revealed

Philosophers such as Plato and Hippocrates tried to comprehend the workings of the mind. Psychologists such as Sigmund Freud tried too to unlock the mysteries of the mind aspect. It is believed that the head is symbolic of intellect, the mind and of wisdom. **Head reveals...** Put your focus into enjoyment and appreciation. Take time out to meditate. Practise Yoga or Tai Chi to bring about peace of mind. Nurture yourself with massages, sea-salt baths and soothing essential oils, such as lavender.

Head

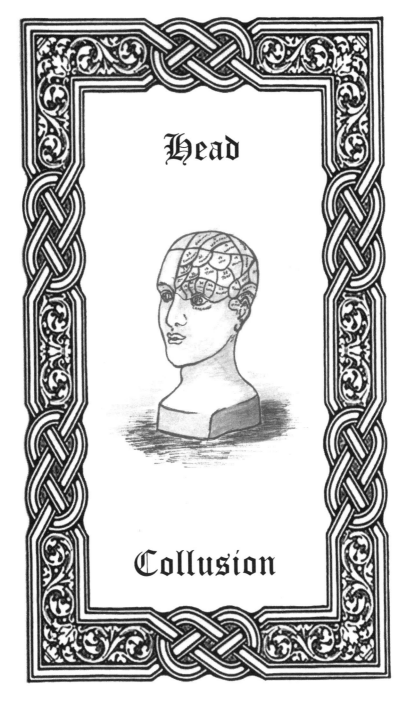

Collusion

16

'In One Ear and Out the Other'

Listen! The universe has been replying to the questions you have asked, but you have blocked your ability to hear the answers that have come to you. You have been asking for guidance for such a long time now, you are focussed on the asking and not being open to receiving a reply. So ask yourself this; do you really want to hear the answer? If your answer is 'Yes', then start to become aware of the replies that come to you. These may be in the form of overhearing a conversation that is relevant to your question, a song playing on the radio, words spoken by a friend or in other ways. Every time you ask for guidance or help from the spirit world, it responds without fail. You are also reminded to listen to others, particularly when they offer help. Be aware that this is also a form of prayer being answered. Make sure you are listening.

Ear Revealed

In Hindu traditions the ear is a symbol of birth. Egyptian hieroglyphics depict the ear from around the time of 3000 BC and it was linked to the circle of life and death. Before reading and writing came into practice the only way to learn was audibly. Therefore the ears were the keepers of knowledge. Piercing the ears was a sign of wealth for the Romans, and for many other traditions, as well as representing a spiritual significance. **Ear reveals...** Take a quiet retreat. Listen to your body, and the messages it is trying to give you. Become aware of what your angels and guides are telling you. Take time to listen to what others have to say. Don't interrupt others when they are speaking.

Ear

Attention

17

'What Goes Around, Comes Around'

Whatever you do, or say, comes back full circle to you and you ultimately face the repercussions of your deeds, whether they were good or not so good. This is a universal fact and there is no escape for anyone. So, now is the time to take stock of your thoughts towards others, yourself and the actions that you take. All too often now people can become swept away with dramas and play them out like some copycat soap opera that's full of vengeful back-stabbing. This will not lead you in the direction that your soul and guides have planned for you. Think first before deciding which route will serve your higher purpose best. This message may also have come to you if you are suffering from someone's ill intent for you. Have faith and know that any harmful deeds towards you will not work out in their favour, and so wish them well.

Compass Revealed

The compass was invented in China during the Han Dynasty, between C2 BC and C1 AD and is the oldest instrument used for navigation. It symbolises the Axis Mundi's circular Nature of Time and is also a symbol of the Freemasons, representing the architect of the universe. **Compass reveals...** You are confused by which direction you should be taking. You are searching for answers to do with your life purpose. Seek the career that you have always wished to have. Take a holiday. Book that trip of a lifetime. Journey deep within yourself through meditation, to discover and better understand the real you. Know that nothing is ever truly lost. Trust your intuition. You have come to the end of a cycle.

Compass

Completion

18

'The Road Less Travelled'

You are at a crossroads in your life right now. There are many paths before you. Some are full of promise to realise your desires, but some of the routes other people in your life would bid you to take are only to fulfil theirs. This is a majorly important time to decide exactly where you want to go and who you want to be in this lifetime, for yourself, not for anybody else. The universe is giving you the choice, which you have complete freedom to make. But ask yourself, 'Which path will lead to wholeness and which path is a masquerade?' Choose carefully and wisely as you stand at this crossroads of life so as not to hang yourself from making the wrong choice. Take the time to make your decision using discernment as your companion. Do not take this lightly as the wrong path could detour you from your destiny.

Crossroads Revealed

This is the traditional and magical meeting place for witches and faeries. The Ancient Greeks and Romans placed statues of their Moon Goddess Diana and of Hecate the Goddess of Temptation and the Crossroads at these intersecting pathways. Corpses of suicides and executed criminals were denied a Christian burial and were instead buried at the crossroads to be abandoned to the Pagan powers. **Crossroads reveals ...** You have taken a few wrong turns. Notice the signs that guide you towards your life purpose. Know that you are always safe. Be careful who you trust. Become aware of others' agendas. Leave a stale or toxic relationship. Be true to who you are. Take steps to discover who you truly are.

Crossroads

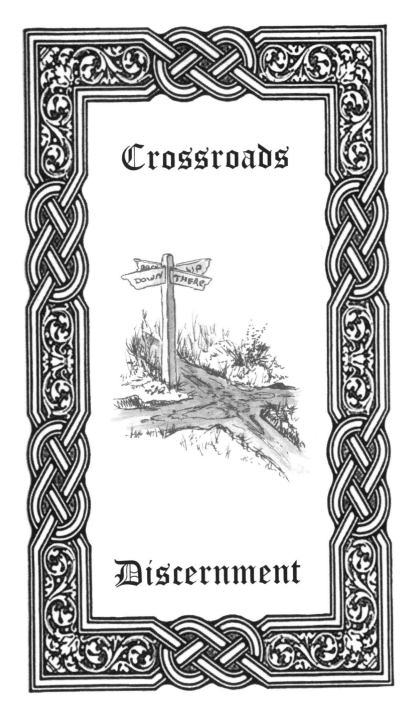

Discernment

19

'Leave No Stone Unturned'

Do not sit back and accept the first answer you are given. You have always taken everyone at face value, and the same goes for what has been said. Not everyone is as honest and truthful as you are; which is something that you often forget. This time there certainly is something that is being hidden from you. Don't believe all that you are being told. You need to find all the facts before you can expect to move forward. You are advised to investigate, seek expert advice and research fully in order for you to piece together all the information. Once you have all the details use them, and your clairvoyant (clear seeing) abilities if you choose, to see the whole picture. That way you can then make your final decision and your move confidently. With all the evidence in front of you, you are able to make the outcome an assured success, guaranteed.

Seer Stone Revealed

Seer Stones are generally made from clear quartz crystal and act as a scrying tool, rather like a crystal ball. They allow the user, often a gifted clairvoyant, to communicate with others over a great distance. They are said to show the past, present and future and to assist in spell work. Seer Stones are mentioned in the Book of Mormon and were used by the religion's founder, Joseph Smith, to receive messages from God. **Seer Stone reveals...** Don't be afraid of using your psychic skills. Take steps to enhance your abilities. Your future is assured. Focus on the positive. Learn to trust your intuition. Protect yourself and your interests.

Seer Stone

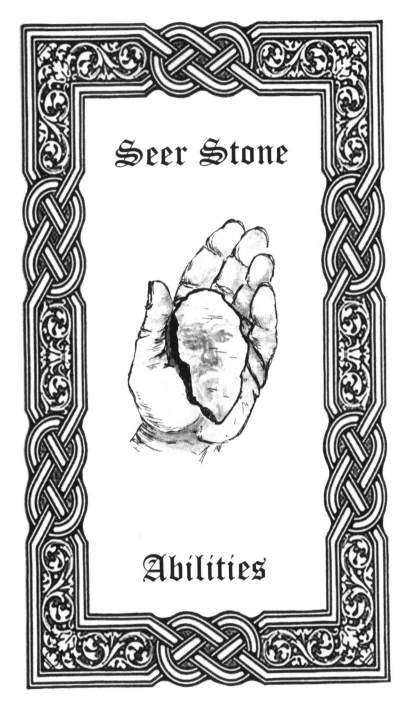

Abilities

20

'When One Door Closes...'

Don't be sad or confused. When a situation, job or a friendship suddenly ends, often out of the blue, it can feel like the end of the world. We can drive ourselves nuts with asking questions such as, 'Why me?' and 'Why did this happen?' or saying, 'It's not fair!' This self-torture often leads to anger, resentment or living in a sense of victim mentality, which serves no-one. Take comfort in knowing that the universe has a special plan for each and every one of us. When something ends it is always for the sole purpose of letting another in that is even better. So instead of feeling distraught or let down, be aware of the spirit world working behind the scenes to bring you something, or someone, better and brighter to accompany you to the next stage of your life. You don't know how it's going to happen, or who is going to come in, but you are guaranteed that whatever, or whoever, it is will be for your highest purpose and evolution. Now that's exciting!

Door Revealed

Doors are more than 5,000 years old and symbolic of the transition between one world and the next. Fairy doors and spiritual doorways were seen as a link to the spirit world. The earliest records of doors were depicted in Egyptian tombs and shown as single or double doors. **Door reveals...** A gateway of opportunity is opening up for you. Allow the old to fall away naturally. Focus on new possibilities. It's time to leave a situation that no longer suits you. Do not act the victim. Embrace the new.

Door

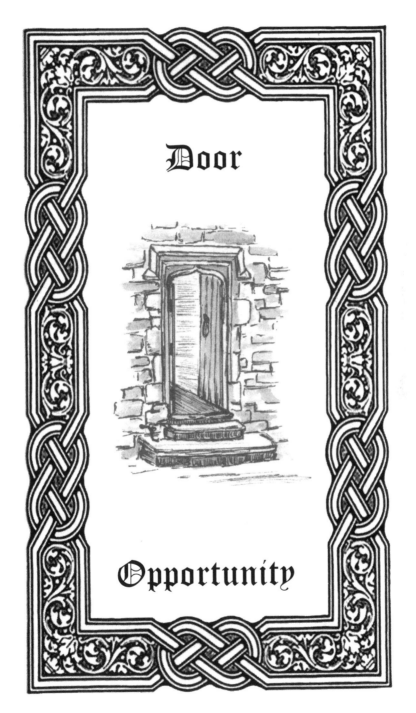

Opportunity

21

'Go With Your Gut'

Your intuition is never wrong and yet you readily discount what you are feeling. It is time to believe in the messages that come to you in the dreamtime, and your gut feelings during the day, because they have never let you down. It is only self-doubt that stands in your way. So let the dreamcatcher do its job to filter out your fears, so that you can move forward and work with the messages that you naturally receive from the spirit world. These come to you often via images seen by your mind's eye, visitations by loved ones in dreams and through your intuitive feelings. The universe supports you as you receive and go on to deliver the important messages, often in the form of premonitions, which come to you regularly for others and often for your own sake too. Don't fear them or think yourself bad or at fault for having them. Nothing will be shown to you that you or the person you are revealing the message to cannot handle.

Dreamcatcher Revealed

Dreamcatchers originated from the Ojibwe Native American tribe. They were made as protective charms to protect babies whilst sleeping in their beds at night. Two spider webs were hung on a leather-bound hoop in order to catch, and prevent, any harm that might be in the air. **Dreamcatcher reveals...** Pay attention to your dreams. Trust the visions and messages you receive. A deceased loved one connects with you in the dreamtime. Learn to control and journey in your dreams through lucid dreaming.

Dreamcatcher

Premonition

22

'Go to Bed With a Clear Conscience'

There is someone in your life who is not all they seem. Someone close to you is playing a game of 'Let's Pretend'. It suits them well to be all that you imagined they would be, and they have had you fooled. But no one can keep up a pretence 24/7 and soon their mask will drop. This message comes to you as a warning to be vigilant and to give you enough time to gather yourself and move on. You have invested a lot of your time and energy in this relationship, hoping that it was leading to all that you dreamt of, but it is to no avail. Ask yourself what purpose does this relationship serve them, what benefits do they reap? Become the watcher and soon you will see flaws in this one who has fitted seamlessly into your life, giving you enough cause to move on and freeing you to spend your valued time and energy elsewhere.

Dreams Revealed

The Old Testament talks of the prophet Samuel who would lie down and sleep in temples to receive the word of God, Joseph who interpreted Pharaoh's dreams and Jacob who dreamed of a ladder stretching to Heaven. The Ancients considered dreaming to be a gift from the Gods and would prepare for their dreams by asking for protection and with prayer before falling asleep. **Dreams reveals...** Give your body optimum rest. Avoid caffeine and alcohol before bedtime. Pay attention to your dreams. Keep a dream journal. Ask the angels to protect you before you fall asleep. Ask for messages and visions to come to you in the dreamtime.

Dreams

Awareness

23

'Lend a Helping Hand'

You are being called to serve! This doesn't mean giving up your worldly possessions and joining the clergy. No, you are being asked to demonstrate kindness, which comes in many forms such as volunteering, assisting someone in a crisis, donating money or even giving a cheery smile to a stranger. No matter how big or small your gesture, you will make a huge impact to those on the receiving end. You will feel better about yourself too, which will spur you on to tending to Spirit's work. If you are a qualified complementary therapist then this message calls you to offer healing professionally by building up your therapy practice. You may feel called to offer healing therapies in exchange for donations for those who have little or no money, or perhaps a local hospital may welcome complementary healing, such as Reiki, for their patients.

Palm Revealed

All ancient cultures practiced and studied palmistry, the art of seeing a person's future written in the palms of their hands. Aristotle declared that lines are not written into the human hand without reason. As you change your destiny, so too do the lines on your hands. Once considered one of the seven forbidden arts of Renaissance magic, palmistry continues to be practiced around the world by gypsies, Indian sages and many others. **Palm reveals...** Visit a palmist. Learn how to understand palm reading. Take care of your hands by moisturising and manicures. Learn sign language to help the deaf communicate. Take up a creative art such as knitting, painting, or crotchet. Give generously.

Palm

Generosity

24

'Stand Your Ground'

The walls may feel like they are about to crash down around you. The ceiling may seem like it is about to cave in. The floor may be rocking to its very foundations and you appear to be on very shaky ground at the moment. Whatever you do, don't back down! Your beliefs are being tested to the very core here and the world is waiting for you to break, which is why this message comes to you most determinedly. Take a moment to look at your beliefs. What do they stand for? Who are you with these beliefs? Who do you become without having them? This is a time for you to stand up and be counted. You are who you are and if something does not resonate with you, then cast it away. Be steadfast. It matters not that everyone else may choose the path of another. You must stand firm and strong, do not budge and your resolution will serve you well.

Pentagram Revealed

In the Tigris-Euphrates area 6,000-year-old fragments of pottery with the pentagram were found. Pythagoras decoded and understood the true meaning of this ancient symbol after cutting into an apple to reveal the perfect five pointed star. In Biblical accounts Eve handed Adam the same fruit, symbolising knowledge and the power it held. The pentagram is the sign of Venus the shining star, who weaves the pentagram as a secret message through the skies. **Pentagram reveals...** You hold ancient wisdom from the natural Pagan ways, from other lifetimes. Study and practise modern day witchcraft and magic. Use the pentagram as a form of protection. Start to tap into your powers.

Pentagram

Resolute

25

'What You See is What You Get'

Have you wondered why, when something goes wrong, more of the bad stuff seems to follow? Or why some people always seem to have everything their way? It's all to do with how you feel about yourself. For example, if you are feeling miserable then that is how the world will respond to you, and you will attract more of the same. If, however, you feel joyous and appreciate all that is around you then you will continue to feel that way because the world will respond by giving you all the good stuff that matches the vibrational energy of what you are feeling and thinking. The universe acts as a mirror, so whatever we put out is reflected back. So become mindful of how you are appearing in the huge mirror of all things, knowing that you will be on the receiving end of the reflection. So turn that frown upside down to change your life around and smile!

Mirror Revealed

The mirror is known as a mystical gateway and portrayed as such in the stories *Snow White* and *Alice Through the Looking Glass*. The mirror is a symbol of honesty and purity, and the Ancient Celts buried their womenfolk with mirrors to keep the soul safe. The Buddhist mirror of Dharma shows past actions, revealing the truth and the path to enlightenment. The mirror that belongs to the Japanese Goddess Ameterasu draws light from the mirror of darkness to send out to the world. **Mirror reveals...** Work on increasing your self-esteem. Believe in your true beauty. Be your authentic self. Imagine a mirrored ball surrounding you and protecting you from lower energies.

Mirror

Projection

26

'Cat Got Your Tongue?'

Speak up! It's time that your voice was heard. For too long now you have kept silent, for fear of upsetting the apple cart. You have chosen to not speak your truth in favour of keeping the peace. The black cat has now walked across your path and no longer can you hide the truth of who you really are. It does not serve you, and the longer you keep yourself contained the more frustrated and prone to dis-ease you will become. Yes, if you speak up it may cause uncomfortable moments, and others (who think they know you), will be surprised and taken aback at your outburst. But better to start living your life now, than living a lie for the rest of your life. If there is something that you need to say, then stand up now and just say it. The truth will liberate you and make space for what is to come that really can help you – and the universe can at last help create what it is you really need.

Black Cat Revealed

Egyptian priests believe that the cat carried magical and magnetic forces of nature. They revered the cat as a deity and Bast was their Cat Goddess. Cats that had three different colours or shades and cats that had different eye colours were highly honoured and respected. The black cat is known as the witch's familiar and as a shapeshifter. **Black Cat reveals...** You will encounter a visit from an animal, as a message from spirit. You have natural magical abilities. You are being protected. Believe in magic. Be like a cat and see through the darkness – of lies and deceit. Speak your truth. Embrace your independence.

Black Cat

Declaration

27

'Home is Where the Heart Is'

Sometimes it is okay to stay within the nurturing and protective walls of home. Everyone is different, fortunately, and the world needs the homemakers, else there would be no one to come home to! You are being asked to honour your feelings, to use this time for some incubation and rest whilst in the comfort of home. Another meaning may be for you to return home to your family, for you all need some connection and healing. Or you may not be comfortable in your own home and need to make changes, either with the occupants, items or a house move. Home really should be where the heart is, whether it is where you grew up, a marital home or the land of your ancestors where you can completely connect. This is an opportunity to take time out and discover where home, for you, really is.

Heart Revealed

One of the most commonly depicted papyrus images comes from the Ancient Egyptians' belief that when a person died their heart was weighed on the Scales of Justice by Ma'at, the Goddess of Truth. This also gave rise to the expression a 'heavy heart'. The heart/soul balance was important to many ancient cultures who believed that the heart was home. It is the very centre of our being for compassion, love and empathy. **Heart reveals...** You are experiencing a sad loss. Learn to love yourself. Give to others. Understand that happiness starts in the heart. Meditate with rose quartz crystal, the 'love' stone. You are very romantic. True love is coming. Send love to those who've hurt you.

Heart

Feelings

28

'This is Your Lucky Day'

Not only is this your lucky day, it is also your lucky week, month and year! Finally all your hard work has paid off. You certainly deserve this new run of luck that has come about through sheer graft, prayers or positive affirmations. You have been blessed by the universe which listens, and the Abundance Faery has waved her magic wand in favour of you. Nothing is standing in your way to your desires and happiness. So what are you waiting for? Go out and buy that lotto ticket, have a flutter on the horses and say 'Yes' to what is being presented to you at this moment. This is a great time to start a new business venture, to shake on a new partnership or to clinch the deal that is being offered to you. Throw caution to the wind and jump in with both feet – you can afford to!

Four Leaf Clover Revealed

The early Celts of Wales used the four leaf clover as a charm against evil spirits and Druids hold the four leaf clover as a sign of good luck. In the Middle Ages children carried four leaf clovers as magical protection and to ward off bad luck. In Ireland it is a symbol of St Patrick and offers faith, hope, love – and give bearers the 'luck of the Irish'. **Four Leaf Clover reveals...** You have attracted good fortune through your positive intentions. The end of the rainbow awaits you. Take a trip to the Emerald Isle. You have Irish and Celtic ancestry. Be aware of the energetic shift that you are about to experience. Enjoy every moment. Resist holding back. A magical gateway has opened for you. Take time out in nature. Use the power of the colour green for healing.

Four Leaf Clover

Incentive

29

'Make a Wish'

This is a magical moment! To make a wish upon a star and for your dreams to come true is the stuff of fairy tales. For the universe is poised ready to answer any wishes that you make. You are blessed with heightened manifestation abilities right now, so take this opportunity to bring about all that you desire. The shooting star has been seen through the ages as an omen of magic and is being presented to you at this time. When you wish upon a shooting star all your dreams come true. This has been written in legends and told in myths since the earliest times. So ride this star through the cosmos, fill up on mystical stardust and know that whatever you wish for, at this time, will be granted. Don't be shy – this is a trip of a lifetime. So grab this opportunity with both hands and fly!

Shooting Star Revealed

The first record of a meteorite shower was shown in 36 AD from China. In one myth, Ptolemy states that the Gods peek over the edge of Heaven and knock some stars down to heal the rift between Gods and humans. Wishes are granted because they can hear anything you say to them. It is said that the wish must be stated as the star is flying through the air, for it to come true. The Greek Goddess of Shooting Stars is Asteria who is the Titan of oracles and prophetic dreams. **Shooting Star reveals...** Make a list of all that you desire. Be careful with what you wish for. Keep your thoughts positive, as your manifestation abilities are heightened right now. This is a good time to make arrangements, take a trip, or enjoy a treat. Release any worries. This is an auspicious omen.

Shooting Star

Totality

30

'Don't Fly Off the Handle'

Simmer! Your blood is boiling and you need to turn down the heat. We all like to have our say and when someone has appeared to do something out of turn it can often be difficult to hold back. This message flies to you, on the back of a broomstick, with a word of caution. If you decide to let off steam this time, it will cause more upset than you bargained for. This situation really does not warrant an all-out war. Trust that all will be resolved without you having to voice your opinion. You may be afraid of having fingers pointed at you, but it will not come to that. So breathe, take stock of the current state of affairs and keep your feelings under your pointy hat. Your self-control and calmness will determine your desired outcome.

Broomstick Revealed

In ancient temples the act of sweeping was a sacred task. Dried broom plant was used to clear and cleanse sacred space. In Ancient Rome special broomsticks were used by wise women to sweep away any negative energy from a house after a baby had been born. Today the broomstick, or besom, which comes from the Old English word of 'besema' meaning woman, is one of the tools of the craft of witchcraft. In handfastings (Pagan wedding ceremonies) the couple jump over the broomstick hand in hand to validate the marriage. **Broomstick reveals...** Time for space clearing. Sweep away any stale old energy or old items that you've been hanging on to so you can usher in new energies. Yes, it's time for a spring clean.

Broomstick

Composure

31

'The Writing's On the Wall'

The time is now! It's no use denying the signals that have been sent from the Heavens to guide you. Be truthful to yourself, admit that it is time for change, and follow this guidance. You are urged to walk in the example of the Vikings and Anglo Saxons who saw the truth in all that was revealed to them through their sacred runes. No longer can you play at being who you are. Step up to the next stage in your evolution. You know exactly what it is that you need to do, and have known for a while now. So leave behind old habits and addictions (either substances or behaviours) that cannot support your advancement. You will find all the support you need from the world of Spirit as you follow your path, marked by signs and signals.

Runes Revealed

The word 'rune' comes from the Old English and Norse, meaning mystery, secret, or whisper. The Christian church destroyed many inscriptions of the oldest script symbols of the runes. The God Odin brought the runes to mankind after hanging upside down for nine days on the great ash tree Yggdrasil, until he saw the runic symbols reflected in the water below. Made of wood, stone, leather or crystals, runes are imbued with the magic and mystery of the spirit of the Earth. **Runes reveals...** You are being called to work with the runes. Your life purpose is to write. Learn a new language. You are a natural communicator. Write that important letter. Spend time in nature connecting with the spirit of trees. Visit an historic site with Viking connections such as Maeshowe on Orkney, Scotland, or the city of York (Jorvik) in England. You have a past life connection with the Norse or Anglo Saxon way.

Runes

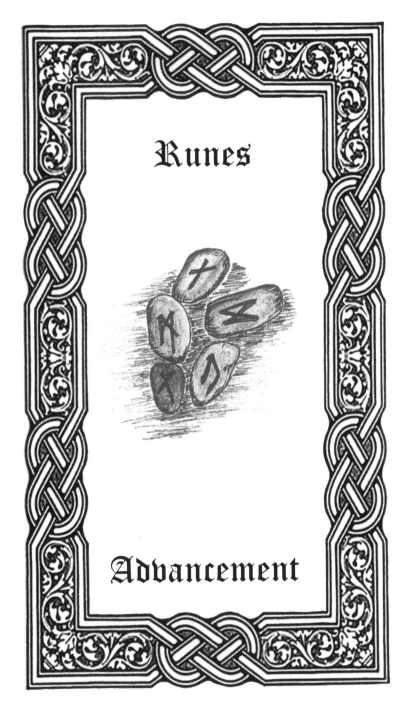

Advancement

32

'See the Real You'

It is time to reveal the real you. You know who that is, but does anybody else? You are desperate to be who you really are. But, having played this facade for too long now, you actually go out of your way to be who others expect you to be. You no longer wish to wear the mask, but are reluctant to let it go. What would happen if you dropped the mask? It would reveal that you are not really who you appeared to be. But how would those still wearing their masks react if you stopped being the people pleaser, the entertainer, the all things to everyone? How would you feel if these mask-wearers treated you differently than when you wore the mask? Ask yourself these questions and do not be afraid to admit the truth in your answers. Only you can then decide whether you are brave enough to show your face and be your authentic self or continue to hide within a world of deception.

Mask Revealed

Masks are worn figuratively in everyday life, to hide the real person. In ancient Greece and Roman times plays were performed using masks. Still today twin masks of tragedy and comedy represents drama. Shamans of ancient cultures used, and still use, masks to block out their identity to allow their spirit guide, animal, or deity to come through. Masks are used in carnivals, and in rites of passage to help transition from the ego to pure spirit. **Mask reveals...**You are experiencing jealousy and envy. You have an admirer. Focus on your own individual and creative style. Step away from gossip. Determine who is a true friend. Look past outwardly appearances. Don't follow the crowd.

Mask

Deception

33

'To Err is Human, To Forgive Divine'

Please forgive. Too much energy has been given to being hurt, disappointed and angry. This doesn't let the person, or situation off the hook, but releases you from the burdens that come when refusing to forgive before it consumes you. So do yourself a favour and bring great blessings to you and your life. Invite Pegasus in to clear away any darkness that has developed within your heart from the situation and then ask him to fill it with unconditional love. As your heart heals imagine yourself being lifted onto the back of Pegasus. As you both fly past the stars you feel the love of the universe encompassing you and all lower emotions dissolve leaving you feeling wonderful and ready to start anew. As Pegasus returns you to where you started from, give thanks to him and see with new eyes all that you have in your amazing life.

Pegasus Revealed

From Greek mythology, Pegasus is a white winged horse who was born of Poseidon and Medusa. He is completely pure of heart and symbolises wisdom and the immortality of the soul. Some pictures show Pegasus as a unicorn. He exudes high vibrational spiritual energy, which radiates from his spiralled horn that's situated on his forehead and offers it as healing to those in need. **Pegasus reveals...** You have a natural connection with the mythological flying horse and with unicorns. You are a powerful healer. Rise above all problems and difficulties. Put your boundaries into place. Ask Pegasus to heal any un-forgiveness that you are holding in your heart. Go horse-riding. Your life purpose involves working with and healing horses.

Pegasus

Heavenly

34

'Time to Grieve'

Let go of your sorrow and have a good cry. Please do not hold it in any longer. For it does not serve you well to bottle up your feelings. You are experiencing a great loss right now and it is important to be able to acknowledge your grief with the drops of your tears. Allow them to flow and to cleanse away your hurt emotions. Your heart has been bruised and you are in need of some gentle healing. Receive some kindness and accept that this is a time to take care of yourself. Call upon the wisdom of the Crone aspect of the Goddess. This wise woman can comfort you, nurture and protect you through your time of mourning. She can enable you to recognise that you are not your emotions, nor bound to them. But before you are able to master this great teaching you need to release and clear. So armed with a big box of tissues, cry yourself a river. You will feel so much better.

Crone Revealed

The wise woman, the elder, carries the wisdom and knowledge combined with deep spirituality and is highly respected by indigenous tribes, and in times gone. Our society today dismisses women as they mature. It is the final stage of the Triple Goddess – from Maiden to Mother and finally Crone, and represents a woman's development from birth to death. **Crone reveals...**You are suffering from a broken heart. Do not rush your recovery. Be kind to yourself. It is important to release your emotional pain. Discover the wisdom that lies within you and allow it to surface. Connect with the Crone aspect of yourself. Accept the ageing process and embrace who you are becoming.

Crone

Clearance

35

'Turn Over a New Leaf'

Oh dear, you've done it again! You don't mean to, but can't you see that every time it sets you back? So enough is enough, it's time to change your ways so that you can move forward, grow and stand in your true strength. Old habits die hard, so if you find yourself reverting to the old ways, don't be too tough on yourself. But it is time to become conscious of every thought and also every action that you make. When you find yourself in this state of awareness you are in a position to recognise that you actually create your own destiny. Make sure it is one for the better as you observe the appropriate thoughts and actions to take just before you make them. From a tiny acorn grows the mighty oak. You are being urged to take this opportunity to grow in the right direction as you turn over a new leaf and focus on your strengths and positivity.

Oak Tree Revealed

The mighty oak is regarded as the king of all trees. Sacred to the Druids, this tree is revered for its great longevity, standing for hundreds of years and is a symbol of strength and protection. The famous oak grove at Dodona in Greece was home to the birds that carried messages to the Gods from the priestesses of the temple. Before temples and shrines were created the Gods were worshiped under the oak tree. **Oak reveals...** Recognise challenges as an opportunity to grow. Stand your own ground. You are blossoming beautifully, don't give up. This is a good time to start a new project. See success in all that you do. A significant anniversary approaches. Release the old so that the new can come in.

Oak Tree

Growth

36

'Watch Your Back'

Watch out! You need eyes in the back of your head. This message comes to you as a warning. Sad to say, but there are people in your life, at the moment, who are not being true to you. You have become the victim of slander and need to protect yourself from much backstabbing that is occurring right now. You are wise to be watchful and to trust no-one at this time. Instead, keep yourself to yourself and focus on your ultimate goal. Do not buy into the fear and the chaos that is being stirred up around you. You know the truth, so stand strong in being true to who you are. Visualise a huge bubble of bright white light around you to protect yourself from any etheric daggers or knives that may be coming your way. Standing strong in the light will reveal what is hiding in the darkness and the perpetrators will be banished once and for all.

Eye of Horus Revealed

This Egyptian occult symbol is predominately of protection. The Eye of Horus, aka the Eye of Ra, also represents royal power, restoration, healing and seeing the truth in all situations. In Ancient Egypt funerary amulets of protection were often made in the shape of the Eye of Horus to ward off evil. Painted on the side of Egyptian funerary caskets, they enabled the corpse to see its way to the afterlife. **Eye of Horus reveals...** Your feelings about this situation are accurate. Spirit is supporting you. You and your loved ones are being protected from any harm. Walk away from sceptics and critics. Use your spiritual sensitivity to see the full truth. Study the use of sacred symbols.

Eye of
Horus

Banish

37

'Safe Harbour'

It has been so tough! You have endured the roughest ride of your life but the good news is that land is in sight. This message has come at this time to assure you that the worst is behind you and you can begin to breathe slowly and surely, knowing that you will never have to go through such difficulties again. You are still shaken from being tossed and torn, so drop your anchor and root yourself deeply into the Earth. It hasn't been easy, but now you can enjoy the calm after the storm. Sometimes we have to undergo a journey of turmoil in order to find that haven of peace on the other side. This peace awaits you now. So go and rest your weary head, knowing that it is over – finally.

Anchor Revealed

The anchor has been a symbol of safety since ancient navigation times, securing many ships in storms and high seas. The anchor became a symbol of Christianity as the anchor of the soul and ranks among the most ancient of Christian symbols, dating from the end of the first century. The anchor was a key symbol placed on catacombs with messages of hope. The first king of Seleucia was born with a birthmark of an anchor; it became a royal emblem and appeared on their coins until 100 BC. **Anchor reveals...** You are protected from harm. Release all negative thoughts, doubts and worries. Ground and centre yourself to prevent you being thrown off balance. Settle down. You will be moving to a new home. Secure and protect your property. Meditate to bring about a sense of peace and wellbeing.

Anchor

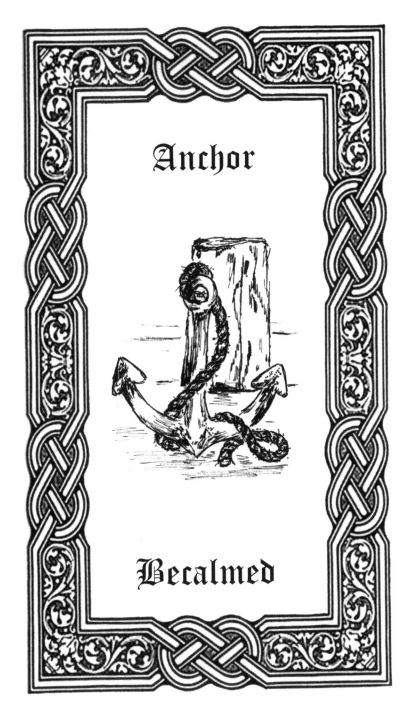

Becalmed

38

'Beware the Enemy Within'

Why do you always make things so difficult for yourself, especially when others try to lend a helping hand? This is a time for you to look deeply within and realise that you are not actually surrounded by people who are against you. The truth of the matter is that you have more support than you care to admit. It is you who is preventing all the good that is waiting to be bestowed upon you. You have a tendency to sabotage anything good that comes your way, as a form of protecting yourself from losing that which means something to you. So you, whether consciously or not, do a good job yourself in getting rid of all those who genuinely want to help. So why not open up, and let some of the good stuff in? It is time to knock down that hard fortress you have built around yourself and let down the drawbridge. You will find that life is so much easier when you stop battling and realise that you don't have to go it alone.

Castle Revealed

From the walls of Babylon, to the stronghold of Ashur, walls, towers and moats have surrounded cites and palaces from recorded history. These ancient fortifications were used as defence against outsiders. **Castle reveals...** It is safe for you to allow others into your life. Accept help from those who are offering assistance. Do not allow pride to stand in your way. Balance your energies of giving and receiving. Let go of criticism and judgements of yourself and others. Throw a party. Invite friends around for a get together. Learn how to soften around the edges. Resist resisting once and for all.

Castle

Undertaking

39

'A Bridge Too Far?'

Don't get swept away! Everything is running along nicely and is working out in perfect time. You seem to have tendencies to go one step too far, before you or anyone else is ready. It is often too much too soon, whatever the situation. This is why things don't always turn out the way you hope for. You love everything to be 'just so' and have tendencies to be a romantic idealist, forgetting that this isn't always the way of the world. You have the best of intentions, which is plain to see, but just rein it in a bit, okay? There is nothing wrong in focussing on biggest and best, but relinquish the need to control. Allowing all to unfold naturally will ensure that the outcome will turn out in perfect order and, more often than not, better than could have been imagined

Bridge Revealed

The first bridges were made by nature; a fallen log crossing a stream or rocks as stepping stones. The ancient Romans were famous bridge builders, as well as building aqueducts to carry water. Many cultures believe that the bridge to Heaven is watched over by a guardian who will either help or hinder those who attempt to cross it. The oldest bridge in the world was built thousands of years ago linking India with Sri Lanka. It was called Rama's bridge. **Bridge reveals ...** Don't rush into things. Have patience. This is a time of gathering information. Learn how to enjoy living in the present. Trust. Everything is working out perfectly. You are on the right path. Your prayers are being answered.

Bridge

Extention

40

'Silence is Golden'

Ssshhh! This is a time for quiet, a time for reflection, to be still. Your days are so often filled with running around here, there and everywhere. Your head is brimming with constant internal chatter. It is time to slow down. Stop thinking about what you and everybody else needs, or could be doing, and take some time out! It is vitally important that you give yourself a chance to be silent in order to hear the loving messages that your guides are trying to give you, to feel Spirit and to notice the beauty that is all around you. Be still, breathe and go deep to the cave within. In this sacred place you will find restoration of balance and harmony. Once you have convalesced in tranquillity you will be able to see with new eyes, and experience every moment that is the gift of life, as you learn to live in the present.

Cave Revealed

Caves have been used by humans since the beginning of time for shelter. They became our first homes where people recorded their time with amazing rock drawings and designs. Many prophets, seers and shamans throughout history have journeyed into caves to seek solitude, to receive their power from the rocks and mountains where the spirits reside. Caves are symbolic of the womb of the mother Goddess and lie beneath temples and sacred sites all around the world. **Cave reveals ...** Change your routine. Take some time out of your busy schedule. Practise meditation. You are being called to work in a spiritual aspect. Down tools and retreat. Spend time alone in nature. Avoid loud noise. Be silent.

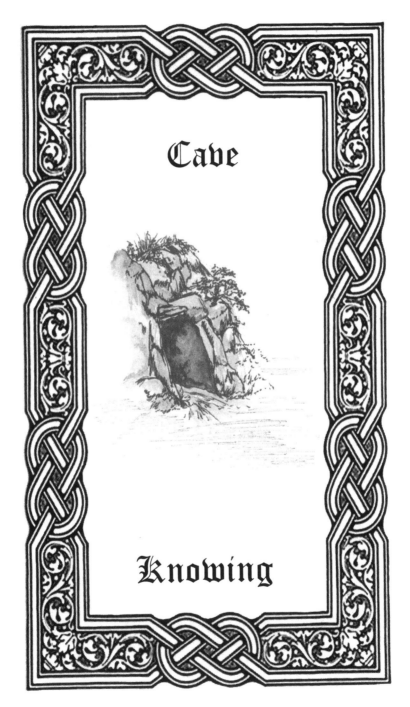

Cave

Knowing

41

'Don't Tie Yourself Up in Knots'

Calm down. You've got yourself into a pickle and you don't know which way to turn. You are too uptight to cope with pressures at the moment and it's causing you to get all into a dither. You are no good to anyone in this state and won't solve anything by acting like a flibbertigibbet. So stop for a minute and take a deep breath in and out. Take a step back. Chill. When you understand that everything that is presented to us comes for a reason you will start to realise the lessons that accompany each scenario. This means that instead of trying to control every situation or fret and worry about the outcome you can relax. Allow yourself to take a step back and then watch everything unfold naturally and know that all will be more than okay. So put your feet up for once and let those tight little knots finally unwind.

Knot Revealed

Knots hold powerful, symbolic and magical significance. They are used as a powerful talisman and some fishermen still carry a piece of rope with three knots in it for protection against storms. Knots and knot magic are closely associated with witches, the Three Fates in Greek mythology, weaving and knotting the threads of existence. Ancient Egyptians believed that the knot symbolised eternal life and tied a knot in their sandals called the Knot of Isis. **Knot reveals...** Let go of trying to control. Release guilt or shame. Focus on love in all situations. Stop trying to be perfect. All is well. Have a full body massage. Relax and chill out. Enjoy a warm bubble bath. Have a night out of fun. Laugh and enjoy each moment.

Knot

Boundless

42

'The Pen is Mightier than the Sword'

Your natural instinct is to fight, but this situation calls for clever tactics. Just because someone else is playing dirty, doesn't mean that you need to follow suit. Whereas you would usually put up a good fight, and more often than not win, this time you are required to use your wits to assure a favoured outcome. Assess the situation carefully to determine your desired result. Look for equilibrium and justice will prevail. It is time to be the noble knight and show your heroic colours. A new dawn of hope is on the horizon and you are being presented with this unfamiliar weapon of using sense and purpose in order to win this time. You may experience great change, and it shall be magnificent. So ride courageously into a battle of a new kind – there is nothing to fear.

Sword Revealed

From Excalibur to the blade used by Perseus to cut off the snaked head of Medusa, swords have been known to hold magical properties, appearing in folklore worldwide. Our ancestors believed that the metallurgy of sword-making was a magical process, taking earth-born metal to be transformed in fire. The sword was considered a sign of wealth, high status and holy connotations in many cultures. The Samurai of Japan believed that each sword had its own soul, which could possess the one holding it. **Sword reveals...** Don't be always on the defensive. Think carefully before you speak. Work out strategy before taking action. You are sensitive to all things fair and unfair. Don't try to be the hero. Handle this situation with care to ensure a satisfactory outcome. You are safe.

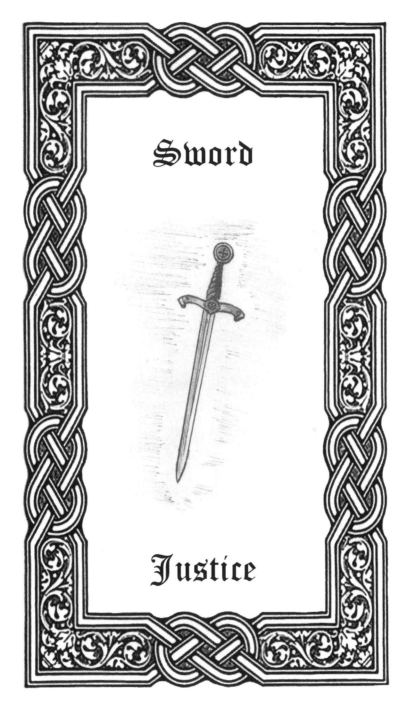

Sword

Justice

43

'The World is Your Oyster'

Opportunity knocks! You are surrounded by a magical energy, and everything that you touch at the moment turns into good fortune. You have often settled for less than you really wanted, for fear of not being worthy of something much better. All that is to change as you now realise your self-worth and that you are deserving of the best. When you fully believe this then the universe showers you with all that you need in order fulfil your life's purpose. Your wishes have been heard, as has your growth in self-appreciation. Never worry that you are being selfish. It is important to practise self-care. So go grab your dreams with both hands and reach for the stars, because the universe is poised to give you exactly what you ask for as it supports you as you change the way you see yourself. Abundance is yours for the taking. Go get some!

Pearl Revealed

Pearls were symbols of love and marriage to the Ancient Greeks and, on a deeper level, the pearl represents hidden knowledge and esoteric wisdom. Pearls are considered lunar, feminine and were dedicated to the Moon Goddess. Symbolising purity and perfection the pearl appears as the third eye of both Buddha and Shiva. Today they are still a much sought after jewel to adorn oneself with in the form of a necklace. **Pearl reveals...** An unexpected and happy surprise happens. Expect a windfall of money. Good news arrives. Abundance comes to you in many forms to match your current needs. Sentimentally look through your old jewellery. A project or venture is successfully assured.

Pearl

Cultivation

44

'Lady Luck is Smiling on You'

Today is your lucky day! You are on a winning streak and every-thing is going in favour of YOU. Have you ever woken up and just known that all was going to go your way? Well, today is one of those magical days! Give yourself permission to strut as you walk down the street, into work, the shopping mall or around your home. You are very special and there is nothing wrong in letting everyone see this. Your very energy will dazzle all those who observe you, rather like King Midas who had the golden touch. You have been blessed with this energy today. So make the most of this good fortune. In other words, grab this fortuitous opportunity with both hands to enjoy the rewards. The Gods are smiling down on you today so roll that dice and don't worry about which side it lands on, for whichever way it does – you can't lose!

Dice Revealed

Dice were used by the ancient Mongolians and the oldest known dice date from more than 5,000 years ago in Eastern Iran. Dice were used for gambling by the Ancient Greeks and Romans as well as knights and royalty in the Middle Ages. Dice were also used as a divination tool by fortune tellers in Roman times, who would toss and then read the dice in order to prophesy the will of the Gods. Over the centuries dice have been made from ankle bones, wood, ivory and metal before today's plastic dice. **Dice reveals...** Unleash your daring side. It is time for adventure. You are on a winning streak. The odds are stacked in your favour. A happy outcome is assured. Regain your confidence.

Dice

Beneficial

45

'Still Waters Run Deep'

Don't dive in head first, even though an offer may be very tempting. You are still reeling from a suggestion, a deal, a relationship that seems to be too good to be true. Have you homed in on your natural intuition or are you ignoring it in favour of your hopes and dreams? This message comes with a warning to you. Don't take this offer at face value as there are underlying issues that are yet to come to the surface. At the moment the situation isn't right for you, despite its appearances. So look deeper into the situation or call in an expert, if the situation warrants it, before you take any action. Once you have uncovered all of the facts then you can decide whether you should take the plunge, or swim away as fast as you can!

Stream Revealed

Streams come directly from the source, from deep underground. They have been honoured as the opening from the underworld and are believed to carry with them the spirit of the hills and mountains. Many streams are regarded as holy and towns and cities have been built round them as a provider of water, and therefore life. **Stream reveals...** Trust your intuition and psychic abilities. Caution will ensure a satisfactory outcome. Your feelings are telling you the truth. Your body is sensitive to toxins. You are fatigued and irritated due to dehydration. Drink more water. Exercise your body through gentle swimming. Take a vacation to the sea, go white water rafting, canoeing or sailing.

Stream

Undercurrent

46

'As Proud as a Peacock'

This is your moment! You should be very proud of yourself. You have done so very well and this is the time to show the world your achievements. Forget about humility, this is all about taking pride in yourself and what you have achieved. Don't hide your light under a bushel; instead shine like the star that you are. Don't worry about what others may think. Be assured that you could be their inspiration. So go strut like a peacock, ruffle your feathers and enjoy every moment of this celebration of you!

Peacock Revealed

This beautiful bird is much favoured by the Gods. The Hindu God Krishna wears peacock feathers in his hair and the Goddess Saraswati is said to ride on the back of a peacock as she writes poetry and music, sharing her wisdom with those who will listen. A peacock stands at the Gates of Paradise to greet those returning home, in Islamic traditions. A peacock feather holds an eye of protection, and so watches over those who wear the feather on their person. In Buddhism the peacock's ability to eat poisonous snakes is a representation of transforming evil into good. Many coats of arms dating from the Middle Ages have the peacock as a symbol of personal pride as the emblem. In Christian traditions the peacock is the symbol of eternity and immortality. **Peacock reveals...** You will receive good news. Be true to your uniqueness. Wear bright colours. Don't be afraid to stand out in a crowd. Others look to you with respect and sometimes envy. Beware of a copycat admirer.

Peacock

Vibrancy

47

'Stand Your Ground'

You are so much stronger than that! Why do you let it happen? You have much strength and yet you allow others to take away your power. When you allow your words to be dismissed, unchallenged, when you permit your actions to be mocked without consequences, your inner light fades because you don't stand up to be counted. Yes, you may say silently to yourself that it doesn't matter, that you know the real truth, but the universe requires you to confidently stamp your authority so that you can grow fully into the 'Wise One' that you truly are, the very soul that others are so desperately waiting to turn to. By standing strong you are in a state of becoming – declaring to the world who you really are. So stand proud, with the strength of the staff, the tool of the ancient Druids as your ally, and step into your full glory, your light and your power.

Staff Revealed

A staff is a symbol of the World Tree which facilitates a direct connection to the Earth. Tribal elders use a staff to serve as a guide and for support, throughout life. Throughout history the staff was held in high esteem and represented royal authority. When visiting England, Jesus' uncle, Joseph of Arimathea, pushed his staff into sacred ground at Glastonbury and it then grew into what is known as the Glastonbury Thorn. **Staff reveals...** Be aware of your connection to the Axis Mundi. You are being called to train as a high priest/priestess, or similar, of your chosen path. You are facing a situation that requires strength. Shine your light brightly. Work in harmony with the Earth. Stand strong in your full power.

Staff

Empower

48

'Stop and Smell the Roses'

You are missing the point! In fact you are missing pretty much everything that is happening. Slow down and take a look at what is really going on around you. Whilst you think that all is perfect in your world, wake up and take another look, because all is not what you have painted in your mind. Question what has been said recently, as well as motives of others and you will begin to see a new picture emerging, that is if you have woken up enough! So what was really behind that funny comment made to you the other day? Why aren't you seeing so much of such and such nowadays? This wake-up call serves you well and asks you to look at areas where you could improve things, or investigate more deeply into situations that you previously skimmed over. Not everything is a bed of roses and you would be wise to watch out for thorns!

Roses Revealed

The rose symbolises love and purity and was dedicated to Venus and Aphrodite. Wreaths of roses were placed in ancient tombs to represent love and beauty, and to carry home the spirit of loved ones. In Ancient Rome a rose would be placed on the door of a room to indicate that matters of confidentiality were being discussed and became a symbol of secrecy. Associated with the Great Mother in India and also Mary, mother of Jesus, the red rose became a symbol of the blood of Christian martyrs and of the Virgin Mary. **Rose reveals...** Love and romance comes your way. You have a secret love. Connect with the divine love that comes from Source. Your heart is healing. Work with flowers.

Rose

Arouse

49

'Birds of a Feather, Flock Together'

Good news! An announcement calls for a gathering, an invitation for many to come together and celebrate. The symbol of the raven is of mystery and magic and indicates a good omen, as it flies with you to flock with others at the celebration. You may find that you have to shapeshift. In other words be who others expect you to be on this occasion, but do not to worry as you will be blessed by doing so. This is a time of joy, of connecting with loved ones and unexpected others. This message marks good fortune for all involved.

Raven Revealed

Dedicated to the Goddess Athena and the God Apollo, the raven was a solar symbol and acted as a messenger. In the Bible story of Noah and his ark, the raven was the first to be sent out to find land because of its intelligence. But because it did not return to the ark the raven was demonised as a deserter. The Norse God Odin had two ravens, named Huginn and Muninn, who flew back to him each evening to tell all that humankind had done that day. Odin had daughters, the Valkyries, who shapeshifted as ravens in order to discover what the Gods had in store for mankind. Ravens were placed at the Tower of London as protectors and it is said that when all the ravens disappear from the English royal castle, the nation will fall. **Raven reveals...** Time for celebration. There is someone you need to appease. Make efforts to keep the peace. You will receive an unexpected visitor. Beware of deceivers. Become who you truly wish to be. You are safe.

Raven

Shapeshift

50

'Don't Worry, Be Happy'

It's time to play because you have been far too serious lately and the stress of this is beginning to take its toll. Life is about balance and you are a little lop-sided! You must play as much as you work; it is the only way to make the most of being on this amazing planet! Okay, you have a lot on your plate and deadlines to meet, but it doesn't have to be that way all of the time. Make time for some playtime. You need to take a leaf out of the faeries' book. They work hard, meeting all of their responsibilities and still make time for play. For they know that joy is the highest vibration of all. So bring fun and laughter into your life, it will bring you more vital energy, you will feel so much better and others will just love being around you

Faeries Revealed

Faeries are magical beings who are the guardians of nature. The ancients, particularly the Celts in Europe and those of the desert lands (whose faeries are named djinn) honoured, revered and even feared the unseen faery realm as they worked in harmony with these mystical beings and the seasons. Sadly faeries were cast into mythology from the early days of Christianity, but are still very much alive as they continue to weave their magic throughout nature. **Faeries reveals...** Spend some time in nature. Listen to uplifting music. Smile at strangers. Laugh at your mistakes. Release judgement. See the joy and magic in all that is around you. Have some down-time. Take a Yoga-laughter class. See through the eyes of a child. Climb a tree, swim, ride a bike. You are the life and soul of the party.

Fairies

Cheerful

51

'Positive Thoughts, Positive Outcome'

The stork brings great news of new beginnings! When the stork flies across your path it brings with it omens of fertility and creation. This message marks the birth of new life, whether it comes in the form of a long-awaited baby or a step in a new direction that will bring about much change for the better in your life. This is a great time to bring new ideas to the table and set about making something concrete of them, as well as indicating that it is a good time to ask advice of others who you trust too; they will be of the right frame of mind to assist you. So get your creative juices flowing and focus on all that you would like to bring about, for this is a very fertile time for you. Keep your thoughts positive and see the best for yourself. The stork will ensure that the outcome of your expectations are above and beyond what you could have imagined as you breathe new life into projects that have been waiting to come into fruition.

Stork Revealed

In ancient Egypt, the stork was associated with reincarnation and the transmigration of the soul, or the 'Ba'. The Ba was depicted with the body of a stork and the head of a human. It would leave the body at night and would return each morning, always at the same time, thus mirroring the punctual nesting and migratory habits of the bird. Today we tell children that a stork delivers our babies – a tale that has been passed down through many generations. **Stork reveals...** There is news of a birth or pregnancy. This is a good time to begin new projects. You are on a creative streak. You will be receiving a wonderful idea – fly with it.

Stork

Expectancy

52

'With Age Comes Wisdom'

Mystery and magic of the old ways beckon. It's time to tap into the ancient wisdom of the ancestors. You are wiser than you give yourself credit for and this message comes to you now because it is time to connect with the knowledge and past experiences that you have accumulated from many lifetimes and engage it all to your advantage. Through the ages you have received great teachings from your life lessons. Now seek the wise teachers who mark the land, such as standing stones, which have been placed at sacred sites throughout the world. These are the great wisdom teachers who have stood silently, witnessing and absorbing every detail of spent centuries. They hold the knowledge and experiences of the ancients in their genetic coding. Spend time out in nature with these gentle giants and allow them to unlock the wisdom that you hold deep within. For it is ready to be unleashed.

Stonehenge Revealed

The stones at Stonehenge were constructed from quarried bluestone found in Wales between 3000BC and 2100BC. Pagan ceremonies were reinstated in 1905. The Ancient Order of the Druids has permission to perform rituals and ceremonies at the site to honour the ancestors and the ancient deities of the land. People from all over the world gather on both the summer and winter solstices to witness the Sun aligning with the heel stone of the stone circle itself, as it rises on those poignant mornings. **Stonehenge reveals...** Visit a megalith site. Celebrate and honour the seasons. Connect with your inner wisdom. The Druidic traditions call to you.

Stonehenge

Advantageous

53

'Seek Your Own Counsel'

You already know the answers to your questions. You always understand what is best for you and the outcome of situations. So why do you spend time running around trying to find the opinions of others? You have the answers already, and deep down you absolutely know it. It is time to trust. The owl sees through the darkness. So take owl as your companion and journey into the dark chambers within, for here lays the wisdom that you seek. As the answers shine forth you will find all the advice and knowledge that you need to help you on your journey. There is no need to seek the approval of others; you have all the wisdom you need at this time.

Owl Revealed

The owl was the symbol and companion for the Ancient Greek Goddess of Wisdom, Athena. The owl was the guardian of the Acropolis and its form was stamped on coinage that came to be known as the Owls of Laurium. The owl was also considered the guardian of the underworld and the companion of the Goddess Hecate, the Protector of the Dead. The owl was believed to be able to cross over to the otherworld to accompany souls as they passed into the afterlife. The owl sees in the dark and was revered as the ruler of the night (also known as the night eagle) and is the symbol of the feminine, the Moon and prophecy. **Owl reveals...** Trust your inner wisdom. You are more powerful than you realise. Take action, don't procrastinate. You are correct. You are on the right path. Don't take 'no' for an answer.

Owl

Advice

54

'Make Hay While the Sun Shines'

Sunny prospects! These are happy days and the Sun is certainly smiling down on you at the moment. This is a time of opportunity and good fortune as everything seems to be going your way. So make the most of it whilst the universe supports you on your path. Enjoy every moment, knowing and appreciating that you are totally blessed and will continue to be so as you put your all into everything that you do.

Sun Revealed

Planet Earth would not exist without this bright shining star. The ancients saw the Sun as life-giving, and thus revered and honoured it as a deity such as Ra, the Egyptian God, and Helios, the Grecian God. In alchemy, gold is the metal of the Sun. It is of the element of fire and represents passion, strength and vigour. The ancient Celts celebrated the full strength of the Sun, as Pagans still do today, at mid-summer and the return of the Sun at Yule, in mid-winter, as part of the Wheel of the Year. Astrologically the Sun symbolises the conscious ego, the self and its expression. 'Akhet' is the Egyptian hieroglyphic sign for the horizon, symbolising sunrise and sunset. For the ancient Egyptians the day began at sunrise when the Goddess Nut gave birth to the Sun in her daily affirmations of life over death (day over night). **Sun reveals...** Your dreams will manifest in the summer. Start each morning with Yoga Sun salutations. Take a holiday to a hot climate. Your sunny outlook draws wonderful opportunities to you. Make the most of a great opportunity that is heading your way.

Sun

Exuberance

55

'Fortune Favours the Brave'

Don't play it safe now! Why are you limiting yourself? How can your dreams ever be realised if you don't dare to explore every avenue? Do not settle for a life that is expected of you, but instead do the unexpected, take up your sword and finally seek all that you hoped would be possible. You are being called to take up a life quest right now. Why not seek out the tarot for some answers, or find a tarot reader who you feel comfortable with and get your cards read. The tarot will map out possible pathways of personal growth and insight and point you in the direction of finding your 'holy grail'. So, once armed with this newly presented information, be brave and go seek adventure and you will discover that wishes do come true. During your journeys you will find a whole new side of you, which you didn't even know existed.

Tarot Revealed

Linked to various mystical traditions from the Kabbalah to alchemy, witchcraft and Paganism, the tarot deck is a magical form of divination that has been passed down through the ages. This ancient arcana has evoked fear in many who have deemed it wicked and evil, and so the tarot deck has been widely misunderstood. **Tarot reveals...** Pay attention to external signs and messages you have been receiving lately. Be brave and face a situation head on. Adventure awaits. Study the way of the tarot. Visit a tarot reader. Do not be afraid to use your psychic abilities. Embrace who you are and play out your role with conviction. A new direction beckons to you. Grab an opportunity with both hands and go for it.

Tarot

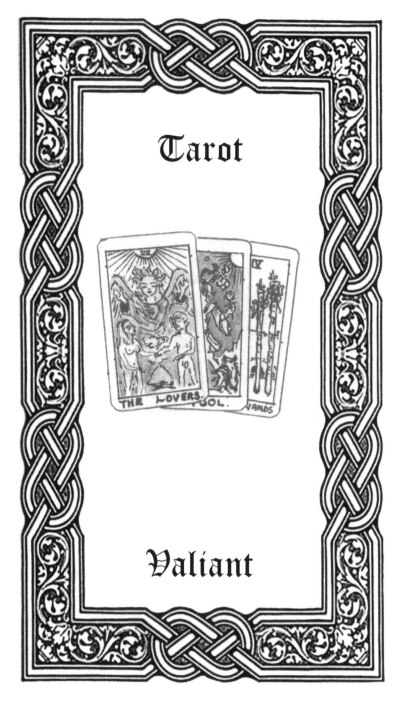

Valiant

56

'Time is a Great Healer'

Relax, your prayers have been heard in your hour of need. This indescribable hurt and pain that you are suffering has taken its toll, and it is hard for you to believe that you will ever overcome this grief. But please know that eventually your heart will heal. It is true that as time passes things do get better. Slowly your heart will begin to knit together the fragments that have been scattered and eventually you will feel whole again. But from today know that there is no need to rush things or feel shame in thinking that you should be over it by now. Bide your time and take comfort in the assurance that you will soon be returned to peace. In the meanwhile rest within the wings of your guardian energy, be it a passed loved one, an angel or a spirit guide, as you are nurtured and cared for. Heal well, dear one.

Hourglass Revealed

Symbol of death and rebirth, the hourglass was first created in medieval Europe, although its origins date back much further with the sand clocks used by the Ancient Greeks, Romans and Egyptians. This measurement of time was used at sea and pirates often depicted its symbol on their flag, to represent the 'sands of time' running out for every human being, to strike terror into their victims. **Hourglass reveals...** You are healing in perfect divine timing. Your natural healing power has awakened. Be open to miracles. Practise Reiki or other hands-on healing techniques. No time to waste, embrace every moment. Quit being a slave to time.

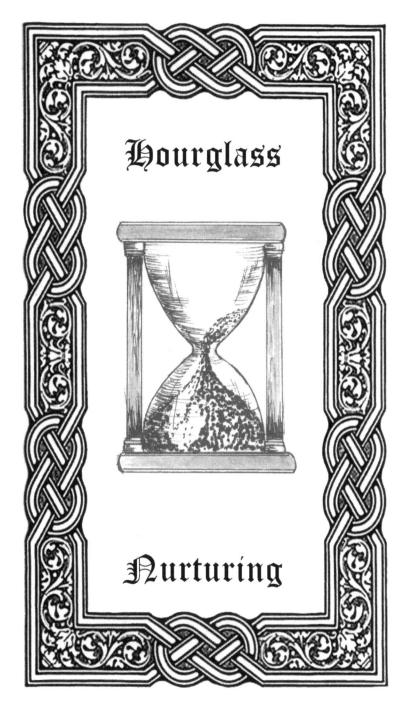

Hourglass

Nurturing

57

'Time Flies When You're Having Fun'

You are having the time of your life – and rightly so! You may come up against others who want you to slow down or ride on your coat tails. Weigh up these requests carefully. Are your wearing yourself out, or ignoring your loved ones? Or is it the acid tongue of jealousy talking? Remember those not fulfilling their life purpose often complain or try to control others. Time goes by slowly for such people and when they observe others are having more fun they want a bit of that for themselves. It is all about the joy of life, without wishing away each moment to reach the next. When we are following the right path, then more of the same comes our way. Grab the opportunities that are presented to you, and go for it. Do this consciously and your appreciation will attract even more good fortune into your life.

Sundial Revealed

The sundial is the oldest known device for the measurement of time and was used since ancient times and by all cultures, in some form or another, to tell the time of day by the position of the Sun. The Ancient Greek Historian of Herodotus (484-425BC) wrote that sundials were initially derived from a Babylonian device, as well as ancient Egyptian astronomy. A sundial is mentioned in the Bible in Isaiah 38.8 and 11 Kings 20.9 as the Dial of Ahaz, and was most likely of Egyptian and Babylonian design. **Sundial reveals...** The timing is right for this new project. Make the most of everything. Stay focused on the present. Live life to the full. Do not listen to gossip. You are flying high; don't let others drag you down.

Sundial

Delight

58

'Once Bitten, Twice Shy'

Well, you will make sure you won't experience that again! Sympathy is with you and your feelings are understandable. Isn't it interesting how our levels of trust reduce when we've had our fingers burnt? So what's this all about? It is a great teaching – understanding that we are not here to rely on others. When the snake is ready for the next stage of its life it sheds a skin all on its own. Our path is one that we too must walk alone. Yes, others may accompany us on the way and we allow them to with love in your heart, but with a respectful understanding of individuality between us. This is the way of mastery. It is a realisation that you alone are responsible for your happiness. So be like the snake, shed any hurts that you harbour, be born again stronger and wiser then glide swiftly away.

Snake Revealed

Modern religion creation myths portrayed the snake as evil and sadly it has been in a hate relationship with humankind ever since. But the ancients worshipped the snake that represented yin and yang; male and female, life and death, good and evil. Indian women would honour the snake in return for blessed fertility. Priestesses of Knossos held snakes in their hands as symbols of feminine wisdom and power. It's linked with sexual kundalini energy – awakening the snake of the spinal column that has been lying dormant within us. A snake with its tail coiled round to the mouth is the symbol of eternity and life. **Snake reveals...** Brush yourself off and start again. Step away from situations that aren't aligned with love. Time for a new look. New beginnings are emerging. Your heart is healing.

Snake

Experience

59

'You Can't Teach an Old Dog New Tricks'

Sit! There is no use barking orders at someone who is never going to be at your beck and call, as you would like them to be. You have tried your best in this relationship, but this old dog isn't ever going to budge! So perhaps ask yourself why you want them to change, maybe it's you who needs to change? Or more pertinently, what is it that is within you that desires them to change? Perhaps it is better to look for the positives in this person, taking them for who they are, and allowing yourself to fully enjoy the relationship with no expectations. If, however, you feel that you are fighting a losing battle and there is no going forward, then retreat. This person is not going to change, so either resign yourself to the fact and build up a new relationship based on this, or get out. The choice is entirely yours.

Dog Revealed

The dog has featured in mythological stories from Anubis, the Egyptian jackal-headed God of the Underworld, to the hounds of Annwyn who hunted alongside the Norse God, Odin. Dogs have a religious significance among the Hindus in Nepal and also in India where there is a five-day festival in honour of the dog as it is believed that dogs guard the doors of Heaven and Hell. For thousands of years the dog has been a faithful companion to humankind, working and living together. Man's best friend indeed. **Dog reveals...** Time for acceptance. Seek solace in a best friend. Prepare yourself for change. Relinquish control. The situation is resolving perfectly. Love your friends and family, warts and all.

Dog

Relinquish

60

'Cry Wolf'

Exaggerating the truth again, making grandeur of all things related to you... If you don't break this habit now, then the help or trust you need will desert you when it matters most. This message comes to you now as there are people in your life, who you love, who are tiring of your endless attention seeking. Yes, you heard right. Sadly this is what it boils down to. You howl for attention and then when no one comes running you fuel the fire. It has worked often for you in the past, but you could be about to get your fingers burnt this time. Look at where or when this seeking attention stems from. This will help you to see that you don't need it in order to be loved, appreciated or recognised. Once this is understood you will be able to move more easily through life building relationships on mutual trust and credibility.

Wolf Revealed

Twins Romulus and Remus, the legendary founders of Rome, were reared and nourished by a she-wolf as infants. The wolf is seen as a fertility symbol by many tribal people and regarded as a strong power animal for its strength, cunningness and protection. The wolf was sacred to Mars, the God of War. The wolf has a reputation of being a loner, rather than hunting in packs. In Greece the wolf was associated with the Gods Zeus and Apollo as a symbol of masculine power, energy and a conductor of souls. **Wolf reveals...** Use integrity. Don't be afraid to be genuine. Stop exaggerating the truth. Seek a counsellor to get to the root cause of a behavioural concern. Connect with your power animal.

Wolf

Credibility

61

'Get Away From It All'

Retreat – it is what you wish to do after all that you have endured. You feel tired and worn out, unable to think properly. What you need is some place where you can be alone, to rest and rejuvenate. You have grown weary of surrounding yourself with the same people and you have become weary of yourself. It's time to bring back passion – to ignite the flame within your heart. Take a holiday or a weekend away. If this is not possible then spend some time alone in nature and allow the healing energy of the plants and trees to connect you again to the joy that resides in your heart. Or take regular long soaks in a hot sea-salt bath. Bathe in soft candlelight with perhaps a few crystals within or around the tub. Once you have indulged in some me time you will come out ready to fight another day with new vigour and perhaps a given gift of knowing your next step.

Bear Revealed

The bear is an Earthly creature and is associated with the Moon. In the stars the Great Bear and the Little Bear are the stellar incarnation of the Goddess of the Hunt, Diana or Artemis, who can shapeshift into a bear. For the Celts the bear was considered a great warrior and King Arthur's name comes from the same root as bear, which is 'Arto'. Bear represents great strength, instinct and intuition. A shaman will adorn themselves with amulets of bear's teeth, claws and skin as magical protectors. **Bear reveals...** You are feeling lonely. Don't hold on so tightly. Seek like-minded people. Know that you are loved. You don't feel as though you belong. Allow your individuality to shine.

Bear

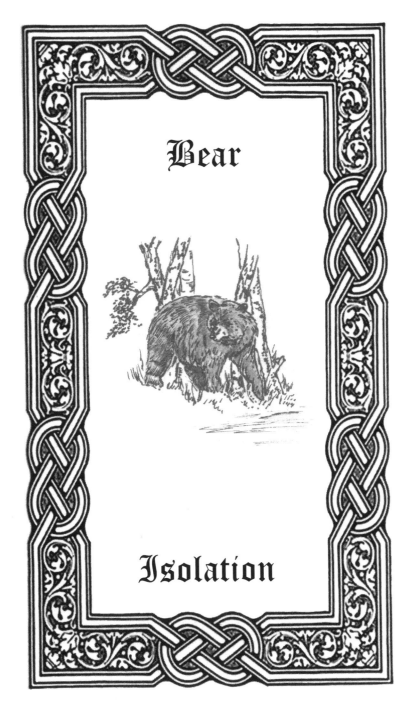

Isolation

62

'Look Beyond the Horizon'

Please don't give up! It is all working out perfectly, you just can't see it yet. It has seemed like a long hard struggle. You have put so much of your time and energy in, and have not yet seen any results to quantify your hard work. You are tired of seeing others enjoying their rewards and yet you seem to be stuck in the port and anchored in the mud. Sometimes what looks like chaos is actually the universe removing things that are no longer helpful to the cause, in order to make way for what is. You are required to trust right now and believe that everything has, and is happening, exactly as it is meant to. What you don't see are the hidden details, what is going on behind the scenes to make it all happen. Please know that all is well and that everything you have done is about to pay off. You are nearly there, so please, please don't quit!

Ship Revealed

The first known vessels date back to Neolithic times – more than 10,000 years ago. Around 3000BC Ancient Egyptians used their extreme shipbuilding skills to create large fleets, as did the Romans and many other ancient cultures. Ships have transported people across the waters to slavery and conquest, from beloved homes and to new beginnings. Today people choose to holiday in ships, in the form of cruise liners. Ships symbolise the bringers of good fortune, hence another old saying, 'When my ship comes in'. **Ship reveals...** Stay positive. Have faith and hope. Your dreams are about to come true. Hold a clear vision of your desires. Have patience. Be like an empty vessel in order to receive divinely inspired ideas.

Ship

Magnify

63

'Rise From the Ashes'

Pick yourself up, dust yourself off and start all over again. It has been tough and you never thought that you would see light at the end of the tunnel. But you made it! This message has come to you to tell you that now is a time of new beginnings. It has not been easy, but a fresh new start now beckons you. So use this opportunity to reinvent yourself. Look at how you wish you could be. It wasn't the right time before now, but having experienced all that you have you are in a strong place to emerge as the person that you would like the world to recognise you as being. You can be whoever you wish to be! So like the phoenix, who dies to its old life, let go of any concerns that may be holding you back, and then re-emerge through the flames of passion, igniting your heart, as you step forward into new life much stronger and wiser than before.

Phoenix Revealed

There can only be one phoenix at a time, with its lifespan being between 500 and 1,500 years. Its home is Paradise and it only comes to the mortal world to die. It takes a journey across India and Arabia, and flies to Syria to construct its funeral pyre before combusting. The next day another phoenix is reborn and rises from the ashes of its predecessor. This is recognised as triumph of the soul over the body and signifies dying to the old and being born to the new. This mythological bird is a symbol of alchemy, fire, purity and divinity and represents the dying of the Sun, and its resurrection the following day. **Phoenix reveals...** A fresh start awaits. You have been given a clean slate. Move forward fearlessly.

Phoenix

Emergence

64

'Don't Get Lost in the Maze'

You must be exhausted using up all that energy by flitting here, there and everywhere! But you don't actually end up anywhere at all. You're like a frantic bee, buzzing around, but not quite reaching the nectar that you seek. Do you even know where you are going? The answer, quite plainly, is no! Firstly, you are spending too much time trying to please other people. When are you going to focus on yourself and your needs? What is it that you ultimately wish to do? You think you know, and try this, that and the other, but none of it is consistent and then falls by the wayside. Make plans. Decide what your goal is, plan how you can reach it, work out a schedule, stick by it and focus! You will find that you become stronger and more grounded as you step in the right direction to reach for what you really want in life.

Labyrinth Revealed

The most famous labyrinth is that of the Minotaur in Knossos, in Greek mythology. Another famous labyrinth is that of Chartres Cathedral, which has eleven concentric circles and a path that is exactly 666 feet long. The labyrinth represents the journey of the soul and the centre is the womb. To reach this is initiation and indicates enlightenment. Labyrinth patterns are found worldwide in most cultures dating from ancient times, inscribed on amulets, stones and the ground. The trail of the labyrinth walks one in a clockwise direction and anti-clockwise to symbolise the course of the Sun and the waxing and waning of the Moon. **Labyrinth reveals...** Time to bring in some focus to your life. Make a wish list of everything you want to achieve. Make plans.

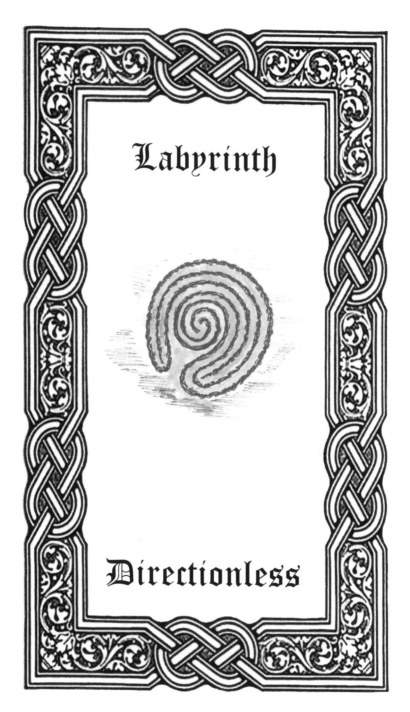

Labyrinth

Directionless

65

'Stay on the Straight and Narrow'

You are heading for a whole lot of trouble. Time to change your ways and/or the situation you are in or you will face disruption. There is universal law called the law of cause and effect. Whatever you do or say invokes an outcome that affects something or someone else. Now this can be good or bad, depending on what you have given out in the first place, and will always come back to its source, you! So observe what you are saying, look at what you are thinking and be aware of what you are doing. If it is not for the highest good for anyone or anything concerned then change it. Bring your focus to that of positivity and then you will make your mark, giving out and then bringing back in all that is good for you and others to enjoy. This is the way to good fortune and blessings for the world around you and ultimately for yourself.

Arrow Revealed

The arrow is of flight, penetration and direction. Eros, the God of Love, uses an arrow, which represents sexual union, to pierce the heart of a sought-after loved one. The astrological sign Sagittarius depicts a four-legged creature with a man's body shooting an arrow, which represents quick wittedness and intuition. Arrows were used by Ancient Greeks, Arabians and Tibetans as a form of divination. **Arrow reveals...** Keep your thoughts focused on your target. Stick to your priorities. Be strong. Don't take 'no' for an answer.

Arrow

Focus

66

'Glass Half Full'

Oh dear, aren't you the pessimistic one! Always looking at worst case scenarios and putting a damper on other people with your negative views of what could happen, if the worst came to the worst. Would you stop it please? As well as summoning up a great deal of fear in yourself you are putting it into others. Do you really think people want to be around that energy? It is so important for you to be aware that whatever you think, and that includes fears, manifests into form. So you bring it into your reality, as well as into the lives of others, if they take on the fears you have shared with them. Do you really want to live your life in fear and misery? Of course you don't. You can change it by simply looking at the blessings within everything and then expect the best possible outcome. You will find that your new positive outlook and optimism will free you.

Chalice Revealed

The chalice is a goblet that represents the power of the element of water used in Pagan and other religious ceremonies and rituals. In Christianity the Holy Grail is the vessel that Jesus drank from when he compared the wine to his blood at the Last Supper. At Jesus' crucifixion Joseph of Arimathea is said to have used the same goblet to collect and store the blood of Christ. The Knights Templar have been searching for this chalice ever since. **Chalice reveals...** Positive thoughts will change the outcome of your situation. Visualize only that which you wish to happen. You have attracted this situation through your thoughts and words. Study the law of attraction. Cleanse and purify your thoughts.

Chalice

Optimism

67

'Get Off the Cross, We Need the Wood'

Stop whining! You really do play the part of the victim so well, don't you? Yes, you have endured experiences that you deem unfair, and in many cases you are right. But it is time to stop bleating on about them. Do you really think that you are helping yourself to move on by reliving them through the retelling of your woes? Certainly others do refuse to listen to these reruns of your dramas. So, it is indeed time to let go of all that has gone and look to the future. See these experiences as great teachings and look for the lessons within each one. You can see how far you have come, how much stronger you have grown and can start by congratulating yourself on coming this far. Now, stand in that strength and grow tall. There is new life to be lived, so go grab it with both hands and make the best of every moment.

Celtic Cross Revealed

The Celtic Cross, known also as the Sun Cross or Odin's Cross, signifies the four directions and the seasons. The circle around the cross represents the planet itself. This sign came about at the start of the Bronze Age. It also appears in the Seal of the Babylonian Sun God Shamash and was also the symbol of the Sun, the king and seen as an access to spiritual powers. With this in mind the early Christians adopted this Pagan Sun sign and incorporated it into the Celtic Cross, which is used today as a grave marker or a war memorial. **Celtic Cross reveals...** See another's point of view with love. Understand the law of cause and effect. Stop acting the victim. Decide how you want your to life to be, and live it.

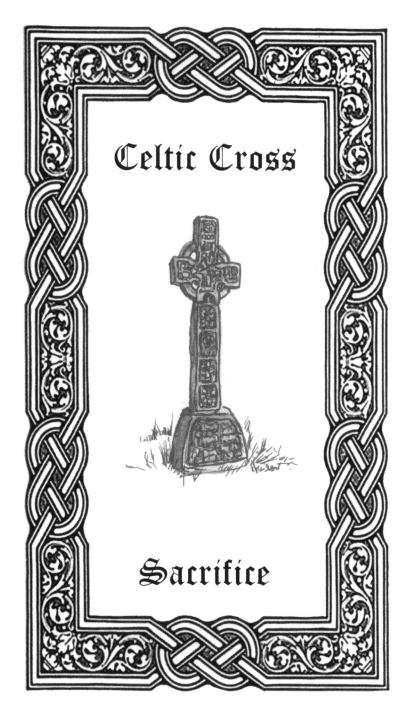

Celtic Cross

Sacrifice

68

'From the Frying Pan into the Fire'

Make haste! You are just in the process of making a huge mistake if you go ahead with this. Already you are playing with fire, but you will get your fingers well and truly burnt if you take this any further. Stop a minute and take a good look at what it is you are about to get into. Please dig deeper and investigate thoroughly before you make the wrong decision. Look to see who this could involve and what effects it could have on others, on you and also your future. This message is a warning and you would be wise to heed it. Look before you leap. Or rather, don't leap at all. You could be licking some very sore wounds.

Fire Revealed

It is said that controlled fire was used from around 790,000 years ago. One of the four basic elements of this planet, fire brings warmth as well as destruction to all that comes into contact with it. Symbolically fire represents desire, passion, sexual arousal, courage and strength. High priestesses and priests kept the spark of life alive by burning an eternal flame in ancient temples. Today the flame of the Olympic torch, originating in Ancient Greece, continues for the entirety of the Olympic Games. **Fire reveals...** Someone is trying to ruin your plans. Beware of jealousy. Explore your options. You are being reckless. Step back and assess the situation carefully. Wait for another and better opportunity to come along. Ask yourself if this situation is serving your highest purpose. Keep your passion alive.

Fire

Temerity

69

'The Winds of Change'

A storm is a brewing and you will be placed in its eye as chaos reigns around you, scattering all that you hold dear. This will change all that you know; belief systems, relationships, work ethics to name a few. Do not be fearful, this message comes as a 'heads up' as it heralds a new beginning. It is time to raise your standards and vibrations to match that of your highest self. The universe has been waiting for you to step into your truth and this is a way of giving you that impetus. Knowing what is coming will enable you to prepare and understand why you will face such dire straits. It is all for the best. You will be supported by Spirit if you stand strong and observe the activity that will be happening around you. Then once the storm has blown over you will find it easy to step forward into the brand new world that your soul has been craving.

Wind Revealed

One of the four basic elements, wind symbolically represents inspiration and connection with the air spirits, the sylphs. The Ancient Greeks had a tower in Athens dedicated to the Wind God and the King of all the Winds, Aeolus. The Druids are known to be able to control the elements, such as wind and rain, by using cloud busting techniques. The doldrums are part of the Atlantic which brings about depression on the weather front, thus bringing about the saying when we feel low 'being in the doldrums'. **Wind reveals...** Be assertive. Devote time to your priorities. Stand strong in your convictions. You may be pushed beyond your comfort zone. You have the ability to weather the storm.

Wind

Volatility

70

'Pot of Gold at the End of the Rainbow'

Congratulations you've found it! But what an adventure it has been! Some of it magical, some of it extremely challenging, but always endured by you with a sense of knowing that you will reach your destination. Well you have done it! You have ridden high through the sky, bathed in the colours of the rainbow and reached the other side where your treasure awaits, the pot of gold, your Holy Grail. So go grab it with both hands and drink its sweet nectar. As you reap your rewards be sure to be in a place of honouring and feeling deep gratitude. For all gifts that are given on the back of Spirit are to be respected, thus ensuring you are wholly safe, nurtured and abundantly blessed eternally.

Rainbow Revealed

In Irish mythology it is said that if one follows a rainbow there is a crock of gold at the end of it, guarded by a leprechaun. To signify the end of the great flood, a rainbow appeared to Noah and it was decided that this would forevermore be a sign of peace from God. Buddha used the rainbow as a bridge to return to Earth. Our ancestors, across the world, saw the rainbow as a bridge between Heaven and Earth. **Rainbow reveals...** Time to reap your reward. Your hard work has paid off. A happy surprise awaits you. Keep your outlook positive. Have a good laugh. Visualise the colours of the rainbow through your chakra points in your body. Time to shine. Follow your heart. Peace is achieved. An argument is resolved.

Rainbow

Endurance

71

'Through the Eyes of a Child'

Do you remember when the world seemed magical? Walking through an enchanted forest, dressing up and waiting for Father Christmas... What happened? Yes, you grew up, but sadly through trials, tribulations and responsibilities that magic waned. What once brought you joy has dimmed as a veil of cynicism now cloaks your senses. It's time to wave your wand and allow the magic to shower you again. It's not just for children, but if you think so then look to them as your teachers. See through their eyes; with joy, with wonder and awe. Connect with your inner child and that mystical world you once believed in. The unicorns are pure of heart, carrying between their eyes a glowing horn that sees through illusion. So connecting with these beings of light will help to open your second sight and find the truth in all situations, rejoicing at the magic within.

Unicorn Revealed

Unicorn paintings were found in caves dating back to prehistoric times. It is said that a magical healing power emanates from the horn in the middle of their foreheads and because of this they were most sought after. The famous tapestry Hunt of the Unicorn depicts this, when he is lured by a virgin and then captured. Queen Elizabeth I paid £10,000 for a unicorn horn, which was the price of a castle. Unicorns seek those who are pure of heart and can be found, it is told, amongst silver birch trees and near waterfalls. **Unicorn reveals...** Time for play. Your life purpose involves horses. Spend more time in nature. Release cynicism and judgement. See the magic within everything.

Unicorn

Magical

72

'Time to Face the Music'

The life and soul of the party, some may say. An absolute scream, full of confidence and always smiling, say others. But who is it they are really describing? It may be directed towards you, but deep down you know that isn't really you at all, is it? There is no point in dancing through life without a care in the world, being all things to all men, but all the while having to hide the real you. For soon the music will stop and your mask will fall. Better to reveal yourself before others do when you are not expecting it. It is your emotions that you need to face, instead of bottling them up under this facade. Leave it any longer and it will all blow up in your face. So take time out to be honest with yourself. You are a beautiful soul and real friends will be pleased to see the real you. So please, dance in rhythm with your life, no longer two-stepping in and out of others to pacify them. It is time now to be yourself.

Drum Revealed

Drums made with alligator skins have been found in Neolithic cultures located in China dating back to around 5500BC to 2350BC. Drums are not only used for their musical qualities, but also as a means for communicating over long distances. Drums were associated with war, as tribes charged into battle chanting to the echoes of a drum beat. The drum was also used to accompany a beheading or to keep slaves in rhythm when rowing the boats that took them to their doom. **Drum reveals...** Be your authentic self. Don't be afraid of what others think. Discover the real you. Love who you are. You will soon realise who your real friends are.

Drum

Authenticity

73

'Like a Moth to a Flame'

This message comes to you as a warning. You are drawn to someone who appears to be charming, such attention they pay you, the sweet compliments they give. Your heart flutters at the mere hint of this person. This person is who you have dreamt of. But could this be too good to be true? Yes! Be warned, they are not all they seem. If only you could see what others notice. You have fallen – hook, line and sinker. Open your eyes before your wings get singed, and fly away before it is too late. This person is not who you think they are. You need to be strong and realise that you have been drawn in with a clever guise of words and actions that are deliberate temptation. If you allow yourself to be cunningly lured by this deceiver you will find yourself trapped in a very different world that you will not like or, indeed, recognise. Resist and retreat right now.

Candle Revealed

Egyptians used candles in 3000BC using wax from plants and insects as did other ancient cultures such as the Chinese, Japanese and Romans. Hanukkah, the Jewish Festival of Lights dates back to 165BC. The ancient Pagan festival of Imbolc later became Christianised and is widely now known as Candlemas. A candle symbolises light in the darkness. Candles, down through the ages, have been lit in every temple, church, house and street to bring light. A candle is often lit for a person who has departed from this life, for the flame can be seen from the spirit world as well as this one. **Candle reveals...** Resist temptation. Someone has not revealed their true identity to you. Don't be pulled into someone else's drama. Don't be fooled by flattery. See through the masquerade.

Candle

Beguilement

74

'The Jury is Still Out'

They say that all's fair in love and war, but not always necessarily so and certainly not in this case. It looks as though you are being taken for a ride and the balance is not tipped in your favour. You have felt that this probably was the case, but thought your hands were tied and there weren't any other options. But there are! Decisions have not been made and there is time to renegotiate. So step back and weigh up the situation. It will mean that you need to summon up your inner strength and face the opposition, but you can do it. Remember the universe supports those who stand in their truth and integrity. So look for the best possible outcome to suit all parties and you can be assured that fairness will prevail.

Scales Revealed

Scales are measuring tools that are used in trade to balance the equality of goods to weights. Symbolically they represent fairness, justice, balance and harmony. The Egyptian Goddess Ma'at weighs the heart of the dead on her scales to see if it balances perfectly with that of a feather. The Hellenic deities, Themis and Dike, ruled over human and divine justice. The Romans then adopted their own female Goddess of Justice, Lustitia. The Zodiac sign Libra is represented by the scales of balance, harmony and fairness. **Scales reveals...** A dispute will be resolved harmoniously. Take steps to protect your finances, business, and home affairs. Ensure that your relationships are balanced fairly. Practise give and take. Learn to bring balance between work and play. Speak up!

Scales

Equilibrium

75

'All Good Things Come to Those Who Wait'

Nearly there now. It has seemed like a long, hard slog and you still haven't seen the glimmer of light at the end of the tunnel. What you have been waiting for, and have yet to see, are the fruits of your labour. This message comes to you at this time because you are on the cusp of giving up. Please don't! You have worked so hard at this and even though you have not seen the results yet, please know that everything is working out perfectly. Certain aspects need to fall into place first. So keep going and as you continue to weave your web be assured that the outcome will be all that you dreamt of, if not more. Don't try to second guess when it will happen, just know that it will. Have faith that all is in divine order and timed just right.

Spider Revealed

Most people are scared of spiders. This fear usually stems from a past life or is influenced by another's dread, such as a parent. It is believed by many cultures that the spider weaves the fabric of the universe. The idea of spinning and weaving is an attribute of The Fates, as in Greek mythology, the Koran and Celtic faery tales. The Native Americans honour Grandmother Spider who has the power to destroy the world if it is not to her satisfaction. **Spider reveals...** Don't give up. Ignore what others might think or say. Stand up for what you believe in. Keep focussed. You are nearly there. Keep the faith. All is well and working out perfectly. Let go of worrying thoughts. Escape from the mundane routine. Take up knitting or spinning. Whose web are you caught up in?

Spider

Perseverance

76

'Practise Make Perfect'

If there is something you would like to do and be successful at, then you need to put in the ground work. Perfection will not transpire at the wave of a wand. The skills you seek will come with practise, practise and even more practise. You cannot realistically expect to be exceptional in your field without regularly practising in order to improve your abilities. Look at the repeated exercises endured by sporting greats who are top of their game. Musicians do the same, as does anyone who wishes to improve or maintain their proficiency. Yes, many are born with ability, but they still have to hone those skills to ensure that they are at their best. Overcome any limitations by knowing that you can do it, you have the talent, and then practise until you have mastered the skills that you require in order to fulfil your true potential.

Wand Revealed

Wands are often depicted as magical sticks used by fairies to grant wishes. Wands were found in Egyptian tombs and Moses carried a wand of hazel. Asclepius, the son of Apollo, carried a wand called Caduceus, with two serpents of healing around it. This symbol is now the official sign for hospitals in the West. In the Wiccan tradition witches use wands to cast circles and to direct energy to situations. Recently the wand has been made famous by Harry Potter. **Wand reveals...** Pursue your true talents and interests. Your life purpose involves whatever it is that brings you great joy. Make a clear decision. Capitalise on your assets. Be bold.

Wand

Enchantment

77

'Fools Rush In Where Angels Fear to Tread'

Whoa there! You could be up to your neck in very deep water if you don't slow down and take a few steps back. Time for you to recognise that your ignorance, or inexperience, nearly led you galloping into a situation without any precaution whatsoever. You misread the situation and did not see the danger sign. Don't be sad that this is an opportunity lost, or feel a fool. Just realise that you were too inexperienced, this time, to make the right judgement. Life is all about learning, and this is one of those lessons that you will be able to draw from in the future. When another opportunity does comes along you will be a little wiser from this experience and will know how to deal with it differently. Next time you will be aware of any pitfalls and clued up enough to know that there is no such thing as a free lunch.

Angels Revealed

The word 'angel' comes from the Ancient Greek, meaning messenger. Angels are beings of light, who bring messages to humankind from the Creator and vice versa. Archangel Gabriel is mentioned in the Bible and the Koran as she appeared to both Joseph of Nazareth and Mohammed. It is widely believed throughout many cultures that each person has a guardian angel to protect them. The Bible tells of a war of the Heavens and a great battle between God and the angels, resulting in some being banished to Earth. **Angels reveal...** Ask the angels for help. Trust and listen to the guidance you are receiving. Your angel is protecting you. Learn from this experience and move on. Have compassion for yourself and others.

Angels

Presumption

78

'Your Task is Not to Seek for Love'

The love that you secretly seek has found you! It has been a long, and sometimes treacherous quest, but one that has kept you searching. Your persistence has paid off. Now you can celebrate as it is time for the symbolic band of gold to be placed on the proverbial finger, to represent the commitment that is being made to you and your happiness. Like the missing piece of the puzzle, this love cements all that you felt was missing. Now you can be at peace knowing that you have reaped that which you always knew you deserved. Your belief in your own worthiness has been upheld and drawn you to this moment. Congratulations, time for celebration indeed.

Ring Revealed

By 16BC the finger ring evolved from the cygnet ring, which was used originally to seal letters. The ring symbolises eternity, the everlasting circle of life. Couples exchange rings for this very reason during their wedding vows. The wedding band, which is traced back to Roman times, is slipped onto the ring finger on the left hand, which is said to connect straight to the heart and is of possible Pagan origin. The ring finger is called the Finger of Apollo, the Greek God of Healing. JR Tolkien's book *The Lord of the Rings* centres around an enchanted ring that brings potential eternal misery to the wearer, and bears the inscription 'One ring to rule them all, one ring to bind them'. **Ring reveals ...** You have met your soul mate. A relationship brings happy results. Love yourself. Don't give up. Come out of the closet. A past life connection is the key.

Ring

Celebration

79

'Things Can Only Get Better'

Goodness, you have really seen some dark days. Times have not seemed to be kind to you and sometimes you have wondered if there was any point in struggling on. But you did and you are here, and you must be congratulated on this. It has been so tough for you and there have been moments when you have not known which way to turn to, let alone who to turn to. But through it all you never did protest. You held your chin up, where possible, and soldiered on. Your bravery and persistence has led you down the right path, you will be relieved to know. On the horizon glitters a much brighter path for you and a lucky break awaits, one that is truly deserved. Your difficulties are behind you now, so hold your head up high, step onto the yellow brick road and walk towards your dreams that are finally achievable.

Lucky Heather Revealed

White heather is said to be lucky for brides, and is popped into their bouquet on their wedding day. It is said that white heather grows over the final resting place of fairies and where no blood was shed on ancient battle grounds. Queen Victoria popularised lucky heather throughout England, through her love of Scottish traditions. Today gypsies sell heather in the high streets to passers-by, to bring good luck. **Lucky Heather reveals...** The worst is over. You are being healed from past traumatic and upsetting situations. Step away from being the victim. A new dawn is waiting. Time for positive change. Luck is on your side. You and your loved ones are safe. Release negative thought patterns. Rejoice in a rosier future.

Lucky Heather

Acquiescence

80

'The Sky's the Limit'

This is a most fortuitous time and you are in a position to do anything that you set your mind to. This message comes to you on the wings of an eagle – biding his time as he sets his sight on his target. With this in mind, take some time to decide what it is that you wish to do or manifest. Whatever you choose will work out well. With the world at your beck and call you might like to take this opportunity to focus on a lifelong dream or ambition. You may choose this lucky streak to travel, visit family and see the hidden treasures of the world. Perhaps you feel called to use your good fortune by working on a community project or helping others. Whatever you feel is right, will be supported fully by the universe. Everything will slot into place perfectly. So keep your focus on all that is good and you won't put a foot wrong. Good luck!

Eagle Revealed

The eagle is considered to be the king of the birds. In Norse mythology the eagle sits in the great world tree, Yggdrasil. To Native Americans the eagle is so sacred that to acquire a single feather is the greatest accolade. The bird is considered so mighty that the Romans used it on the top of their Imperial Standard. When an emperor died, eagles were released into the skies symbolising the soul ascending to the Heavens. Today the eagle is still a prominent political symbol for many nations including the USA, Germany, the Russian Federation, and Poland to name a few. **Eagle reveals...** A doorway of opportunity is open for you. You are flying high right now. Success is yours for the taking.

Eagle

Without
Measure

81

'Pride Comes Before a Fall'

Are you quite sure that enough people know how 'wonderful' you are? Just because you seem to excel at something, or have experienced recent success, does not guarantee repeated good fortune. It's all very well having confidence and recognising your own strengths, but not to the detriment of others – their opinions of you can be damaging, and you have not been doing yourself any favours by bragging. If you are not careful you could lose a few good friends. Tone down your attitude and recognise the abilities and talents of others. It takes a special kind of strength to allow others to shine. This can prove difficult if you have fed your ego to bursting point. So consider others before proclaiming greatness. Remember breaking rungs on the ladder going up, will only make your descent that much quicker and unstoppable...

Lion Revealed

As the 'King of the Jungle' the lion has been revered and feared for its strength, ferocity and might by humankind throughout the ages. It is the totem animal of kings, emperors and Gods. The Egyptian Goddess of War was the lion-headed Sekhmet. The lion is synonymous with the Sun and the Zodiac sign of Leo. Aslan the lion was immortalised through the Narnia books by CS Lewis. He is believed to symbolise Christ and portray the Christian take on birth and resurrection. **Lion reveals...** Be respectful and aware of others' feelings. Be careful not to rub anyone up the wrong way. Think before you speak. Be the observer of your words and actions. Remember it takes great strength to act with humility.

Lion

Humility

82

'Ring any Bells?'

There is something familiar in the air. You can't quite put your finger on it, but this awareness has been playing on your mind. Many senses evoke memories of a distant past – the scent of a beloved grandparent or the earthy damp leaves of an autumnal forest. Music can be the soundtrack of life. Hearing a song from your youth can help you relive that first kiss, a break up, school disco, or remind you of a loved one who may have passed to Spirit. You are being called to reach deep into your past as something, relevant to today, resides there. This is very important to who you are the signs are directing you. Dig out old diaries, or look through the photographs of your childhood and allow yourself to drift back to those times gone by. Soon you will remember what is waiting to be revealed, to be used now. This is also an opportunity to rewrite your story anew.

Bells Revealed

Bells first appeared in Ancient China around 2000BC. They were used in religious ceremonies and traditions. Bells were viewed as instruments of the Gods to carry their will of happiness. Moses studied bells and gongs in the priesthood in Egypt. Parishioners are called to attend services by the sound of pealing church bells. A town crier used a bell to bring notices to crowds or to 'bring out the dead'. The bell would toll to bring a warning of impending attack. **Bells reveals...** Time to investigate your ancestry. Someone from your past gets in touch. Have a past life regression session with a reputable therapist. Become attuned with your inner child. A previous romance is rekindled. Old secrets may be revealed.

Bells

Evoke

83

'Truth Hurts Now, But Lies Hurt Forever'

You are still reeling from a bombshell. You feel such devastation. You don't know what is real anymore and continuously torture yourself with questions. The only way to heal is to know that it is much better to have found out now than to have been continuously misled. No one deserves to be in your life if they think you aren't worthy enough for the truth. You have the opportunity to move on and build a life based on truth. This experience will help you to use discernment in the future, choosing only those around you who have integrity. Know that in time the right people will come along. Affirm each day that you only attract and accept people into your life for your highest good. As you make this bold statement you will grow strong in your resolution and the universe will match your intentions. This truth, however painful, has actually set you free.

Dagger Revealed

In pre-dynastic Egypt, daggers were worn as ceremonial objects as a symbol of power. Daggers have been around since Neolithic times as weapons and cutting tools. Throughout the world today knives are used as religious and ceremonial implements. In Wiccan traditions the dagger, or athame, is used to cut through energies in ritual and ceremony and originated in the Middle Ages. Knives were buried with the Saxon dead so they would be able to defend themselves on their journey to the next world. In Greece a black handled knife is placed under the pillow to ward off nightmares. **Dagger reveals...** Leave a situation you have outgrown. Be assertive. Set your boundaries. Learn from the lessons learnt. Walk away.

Dagger

Elimination

84

'You're Spinning out of Control'

You are driving yourself mad with worry. You fret about every little thing, not just for you, but for everyone else too. But have you noticed that it's mostly about what 'might' happen. Stop! Why are you torturing yourself so? Where does this all stem from? Look at the root cause. Perhaps a loved one had an accident and you have built up a heightened sensitivity to potential pitfalls. The media could be fuelling this behaviour. Realise that whatever you think or imagine is seen by the universe and then matched. So if you are always worrying that you will have an accident, eventually it will happen. Think positively. See yourself whole and completely safe. Visualise a bright white light around all that you wish to protect and keep your words positive. Your life becomes brighter and happier without any of the old worry thoughtforms holding you back.

Wheel Revealed

The oldest wheel is more than 5,000 years old. The invention of the wheel made transportation possible. Symbolically the wheel represents the circle of life. There are many attributes to the wheel such as the Zodiac, the Wheel of Fortune, the eight-spoked Wheel of Dharma to name but a few. A wheel was used often to symbolise the Sun, the Moon and the changing seasonal Wheel of the Year. The Native Americans built Medicine Wheels as a representation of the cosmos. **Wheel reveals...** Similar situations will keep cropping up until you learn from your experience. Stay grounded. Learn to say 'No'. Focus. Retrain your thoughts to only positivity. Give thanks for all situations. Pray for guidance and protection.

Wheel

Continuous

85

'Plenty More Fish in the Sea'

It is always devastating to lose something or someone we loved, especially if you thought that they reciprocated your feelings. Take a deep breath and dive down into the emotions that engulf you. You will discover what these intense feelings really mean. They may speak of betrayal, of rejection, of abandonment, of being fed lies. Now if you swim deeper still, through these murky waters, you may find that you have witnessed one or all of these experiences before. By discovering that this whole situation has triggered past hurts that need to be dealt with, not through the loss of this person (or item) per se, then you are at a very good vantage point to heal. Uncovering the buried pain, understanding its origins and working through it, you will be free to notice that there are actually very many good catches out there, waiting to be reeled in. Go for it!

Dolphin Revealed

The name dolphin derives from the Greek 'delphinos', meaning womb. The name Delphi is from the same root and it was at this temple that the God Apollo arrived in the shape of the dolphin. Dolphins are highly intelligent water mammals and are considered, by some, as the wisdom keepers of Atlantis. In Greek art dolphins are depicted as carrying the souls of the dead on their backs to the Isles of the Blessed. Many people are drawn to swim with dolphins, due to their friendly and fun nature. **Dolphin reveals...** Pick yourself up and get out there. Happiness awaits you. Use your deep wisdom to learn from this experience. Know that you are worthy. Make a date with friends for fun and laughter. Love is waiting.

Dolphin

Bountiful

86

'Ladder of Success'

Congratulations, all that hard work, coupled with natural flair, is just about to pay off. There are no secrets to your success; it is a result of vision, hard work, dedication and learning from failure. Many people don't achieve their goals; they give up at the first hurdle and, unlike you, easily resist a challenge. You have always been one to pick yourself up, dust yourself off and move forward with renewed vigour. You are to be applauded for always applying the best of yourself to the task at hand and now promotion awaits you. This could be within your current job, or elsewhere. So give yourself permission to accept it, graciously, and reap the benefits that are on offer. So be proud of yourself as you take that first step, for the top of the ladder is certainly in sight for you, at long last. All things are possible for those who believe, and you are living proof of this.

Ladder Revealed

A 10,000-year-old rock painting of a ladder can be found in the Spider Caves of Valencia, in Spain, and is thought to symbolise ascension and transcendence between Heaven and Earth. In Freemasonry it signifies initiation and ascension to higher levels of consciousness. The Kiva was a sacred room for prayers, dug deep down into Mother Earth and only accessible by a long ladder through a single narrow opening in the ground. The ladder represented the path to the underworld. The most famous example is Jacob's Ladder. This Biblical character was given a vision of a ladder in the dreamtime, which stretched up to the Heavens. **Ladder reveals...** Success is yours. Release any doubts or worries, for a happy outcome is assured.

Ladder

Triumphant

87

'Beat a Hasty Retreat'

Caution, you are treading on very fragile ground. Back out simply and quietly from this situation. Okay, so you feel it wasn't exactly your fault. But it really is time for you to realise that you must take some responsibility for your actions and the most sensible, at this moment in time, is to get out of there! This situation really is not at all an ideal one for you, and even though it may have all seemed wonderful at the time, you have realised that not everything is quite what it appeared to be in the first place. So this message has come to warn you that dangers are lurking in the shadows, and you are about to be snared. You are being urged to withdraw immediately, and keep away completely, with the utmost of urgency. You are invited to open another page if you feel you need another message to accompany this one.

Dragon Revealed

In April 2013, remains thought to be dragon bones were discovered in the Chinese sea. The dragon is greatly revered by the Chinese, but feared by most of the world. In England, the patron saint is St George, who is celebrated each April 23rd for slaying a dragon and freeing the people from its tyranny and aggression. Dragons are magical beings and are seen as being predominately of the element of fire, as well as being guardians of Earth-based spirituality and traditions such as Wicca, Paganism, Druidry and Shamanic practices. The dragons are ancient wisdomkeepers and offer great strength, protection and courage. **Dragon reveals...** Protection is required. Trust your intuition. Regroup and think again.

Dragon

Unrestrained

88

'Once in a Blue Moon'

A rare event is about to occur. Your life will never be quite the same again and the outcome will be very pleasant indeed. You will fall upon it quite by accident. That's often how the universe brings us what we have wished for. When we plead and plead for our wishes to be answered we block ourselves to receive, because we are forcing the issue. Your requests have been heard and now you are being asked to step out of the way as they are fulfilled. The saying goes, 'We make plans and God laughs.' Well, bear that in mind as this certainly is very fitting for what is in store for you. Things will definitely work out beautifully, but quite unconventionally and not in a way that you could imagine. You may call it a 'happy accident' or a 'fortunate mistake'. Whichever way and however it happens, you will be very pleased it did.

Eclipse Revealed

Ancient civilisations believed that an eclipse was caused by a demon or a dragon eating the Sun. In 585BC two armies were engaged in battle, in what is now present day Turkey. As darkness fell upon the land, due to the solar eclipse, the armies took this as a sign and stopped fighting instantly, making peace with one another. Witches and wizards have been blamed for eclipses, leading to punishment by execution. Eclipses were often seen as impending miracles, the wrath of God, or the downfall of a ruling dynasty. It is said that eclipses played a part in the birth of Mohammed and the crucifixion of Jesus. **Eclipse reveals...** Watch out for signs. This message comes as an auspicious omen. Good fortune is yours.

Eclipse

Serendipity

89

'Absence Makes the Heart Grow Fonder'

Take comfort in knowing that your loved one is not far away. Your heart is where they reside, as you do in theirs. This is where you can connect, whether the person is unable to be with you physically at the moment, or if they now reside in the spirit world. Allow yourself to grieve, there is no shame, nor is it a sign of weakness. Be gentle with yourself, for your heart and emotions are fragile. You might like to set up an altar in dedication to the one you are missing. A simple table with a cloth, a mantelpiece or even your bedside unit will do to place a few photographs and some trinkets. This way you keep a direct link through your thoughts each time you look at it. In doing so your heart will strengthen and your love will grow. If you are grieving for a love that is not reciprocated then draw open another page for the advice that you seek.

Lock of Hair Revealed

Primitive belief maintains that owning a lock of hair from another's head gives one power over that individual. Historically the giving of a lock of hair was a sign of love and devotion, especially before separating for a journey or war. In Ancient Rome girls about to be married offered locks of their hair to Jupiter. Many mothers keep a lock of baby's first hair for good luck. Victorians placed a lock of hair from a lover in a locket to keep. **Lock of Hair reveals...** Time to reflect on your feelings. Be gentle with yourself. Catch up on some sleep. Stay away from harsh negative situations or people. Listen to some peaceful music.

Lock of Hair

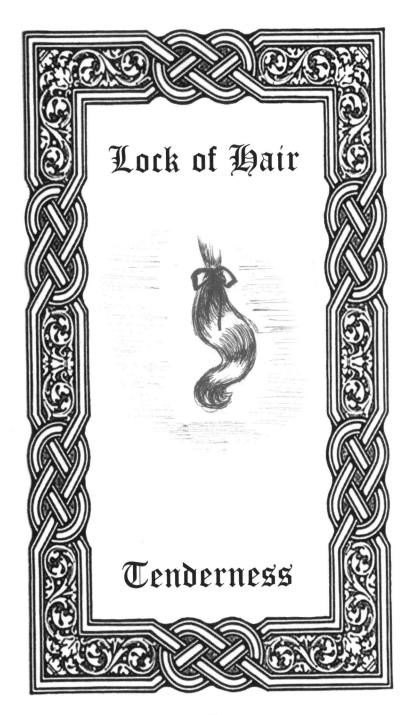

Tenderness

90

'Skeleton in Your Closet'

You have been hiding something from others, and for a long time. But doors tend to be opened at some point and when the secret is out it will appear much worse than originally. And this is because it has been deliberately hidden whilst you have been living a lie. The longer the lie continues, the bigger it grows and when the truth gets out, you will regarded as a stranger by all who knew you. Now, ask yourself this, if you discovered that a friend had been keeping a secret from you, what would be more hurtful – the hidden truth, or that fact that the person didn't feel they could be open and honest with you? It would be much better, for you, if you came clean right now. Yes, it may be scary to stand up and be counted, but by doing so you will be understood more readily than if your dark secret was uncovered in another way. Face up to your past or be exposed and lose face. The choice is yours – you hold the key.

Key Revealed

The first key was discovered in Ancient Assyria. Clay tablets from Babylonia depict keys, which were found 4,000 years ago. In Ancient Greece keys were used for temples and Spartan locks were renowned. Women were the keeper of the keys. Keys were buried with the dead in order that the doors to the underworld would open easily. Our ancestors used a physical key as a magical charm or talisman. The key is the symbol of power. To be given the keys to a town or city is a great honour and a granting of power. Today the symbolic 'key of the door' is still given on a 21st or 18th birthday. **Key reveals...** Time to be honest with yourself and others. Be integral in all that you do. Be honest.

Key

Honesty

91

'Blow Your Own Trumpet'

You did it! Well this is certainly a time to celebrate and let the world know how well you did. So hang out the bunting, wave the flags and make a great big song and dance about it, because you rightly deserve this moment. It has been a long time coming, and you have been waiting for this for what has seemed an age. Your natural tendency is to hold back and allow others to enjoy the limelight. Where a little humility and humbleness has done you credit in the past, it will not cut it this time. This is your moment and at long last you can show the world exactly what you are made of. This is a great achievement, made through dedication, luck, good fortune and sheer skill. You always knew you had it in you and that you could do it. So it's about time others realised what a talent you are. Don't shrink back this time, enjoy your moment. It is time to take off the invisibility cloak and stand tall. Let the fanfare commence!

Trumpet Revealed

It is believed that the trumpet was used as a signalling device for the Ancient Egyptians and Greeks as well as in the Middle East. Trumpets date back to 1500BC and were found in Tutankhamen's tomb. Trumpets were often used as an announcement, often for royalty and in battle. Archangel Gabriel is depicted with a golden trumpet. She is the messenger angel who announced the impending birth of Jesus to Joseph and the actual birth itself to the shepherds, according to the Bible. **Trumpet reveals...** Time to celebrate. Good news arrives. Be proud of who you are and your achievements.

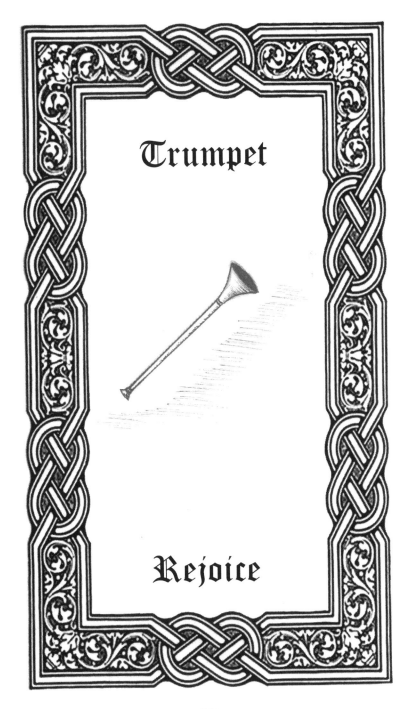

Trumpet

Rejoice

92

'Seek Wise Counsel'

It is time to let go and admit defeat. Why do you insist on trying to do it all by yourself, you just don't like being told, do you? You may wish to be seen as the brightest and the best, but even those who have attained mastery will never confess to being this. Life brings new lessons and experiences and if there is someone who has already 'been there', then why not learn from them to help you on your way? This was always the way of the ancients who would make homage to a wise person to receive insight and clarity and then take appropriate action. You are being asked to do the same. Maybe seek out a respected tarot reader, medium or counsellor. You will not be judged. Heeding wisdom from one who is knowledgeable is a sign of strength. If you allow yourself to surrender then you will have achieved the first steps towards mastering acceptance.

Oracle Revealed

An oracle is one who gave wise counsel and predictions. The Ancient Greeks sought advice of the oracle, Pythia, at the temple in Delphi, who only gave prophecies on the 7th day of each month. In these male-dominated societies it was women who were the oracles. Today the Dalai Lama is the official state oracle of Tibet. Divination cards, similar to the tarot deck, are called oracle cards, for they give wise advice in the form of written word or a picture. **Oracle reveals...** Visit a reputable clairvoyant. Ask for guidance and signs. Don't let pride stand in your way. Keep an open mind. The wisdom you seek comes from within. Draw and learn from your experiences. Share your knowledge with others.

Oracle

Mastery

93

'A Fish out of Water'

You have been subjected to an abuse that your body can no longer contain, affecting you spiritually, physically or emotionally. Your energetic flow is clogged. If you work with others who bring you down with their negative attitudes and vile gossip then you must protect yourself. Picture being surrounded by a white light or visualise a shield of mirrors reflecting back anything unpleasant. Carry a grounding crystal, such as black tourmaline or hematite, as a buffer. This message could also indicate a nutritional abuse of your body affecting your metabolism and lowering your energetic vibration. Reduce any intake of alcohol, caffeine and fatty/sugary foods. Combine this with an awareness of natural healing practices, e.g. connecting with seashells which are continuously imbued with the healing energy of starlight and cleansing properties of the ocean.

Seashell Revealed

Seashells are strung together and worn as jewellery and necklaces by women, men and by mermaids. Seashells are used to listen to the waves of the sea. They have been used for divination purposes and also as healing tools, much like crystals. Seashells have been used as wind instruments for years, such as large sea snail shells making what is known as the conch. The Pearly Kings and Queens of London's East End have their gowns covered head to toe in pearly shell buttons. **Seashell reveals...** Clean up your act. Purify and cleanse your spirit by indulging in a sea salt bath. Keep your thoughts clear and purified. Engage in purification rituals involving water. Take a vacation near the ocean. Heal with seashells.

Seashell

Purification

94

'Don't Put All Your Eggs in One Basket'

Keep your options open! Please look at alternatives, at this time, because you may just lose everything. These words are not written to worry you, but to instil some common sense. It is never wise to invest all that you have in only one possibility. It is a good idea to seek advice from an expert or chat with a friend before you make up your mind. When King Edward IV died, both his young sons, who were the next heirs to the throne of England, were summoned to the Tower of London. Their mother, Elizabeth Woodville, is rumoured to have sent another boy in place of one of the sons. This was a careful and clever decision so that if anything untoward were to happen to the boys, then at least one prince would be safe. This was a shrewd move by a wise woman, and a story that you may like to remember as you make any decisions that could affect yourself or others.

Egg Revealed

In Ancient Egypt eggs were hung in temples to encourage fertility. In Christianity and Paganism eggs represent resurrection. The egg is used to celebrate Easter by the Christians, an idea adopted from the Pagans who honoured the Goddess Ostara, who brought about new life and fertility. In the Middle Ages, and later, stories of eggs abounded, such as 'The Goose Who Laid the Golden Egg', a dream for most poor families at that time. The Celts, Hindus, Egyptians and Greeks all embrace the symbol of the World Egg that rose from the primeval waters, and from which the universe is said to have hatched. **Egg reveals...** Keep your options open. Explore alternative routes before making any decisions. Seek advice.

Egg

Options

95

'Never Judge a Book by its Cover'

Appearances can be deceptive. When you first meet someone, what is it that you are seeing – external looks or something deeper, revealing who the person really is? You are in danger of mistaking someone, quite prevalent, for being very different to what they are really all about. This person may appear to look the part, but are they really? You certainly have believed them and have been rather misled. Use discernment to distinguish between who is the 'real deal' and who is a pretender. You may like to look at how you appear to other people. Do you allow yourself to come across as you really are? It is important for you to be genuine. There are people who won't be fooled by the personification that you so desperately wish to convey and you will be in danger of being publicly exposed. Think twice, because you can't keep pulling the wool over everyone's eyes.

Book Revealed

Books were created to document records and history. They were originally written on stone, clay and then wood which led to the making of papyrus, the first paper. Book production was developed in Rome in the 1st Century BC and bookstores were available throughout the Roman Empire. In 377AD there were 28 libraries in Rome. Throughout the years and all over the world many important libraries, such as the Library of Alexandria, were burned and destroyed to wipe out ancient esoteric secrets and knowledge of the old ways. **Book reveals...** It is important to be genuine. Learn to love the real you. Don't be fooled by illusions. See the bigger picture.

Book

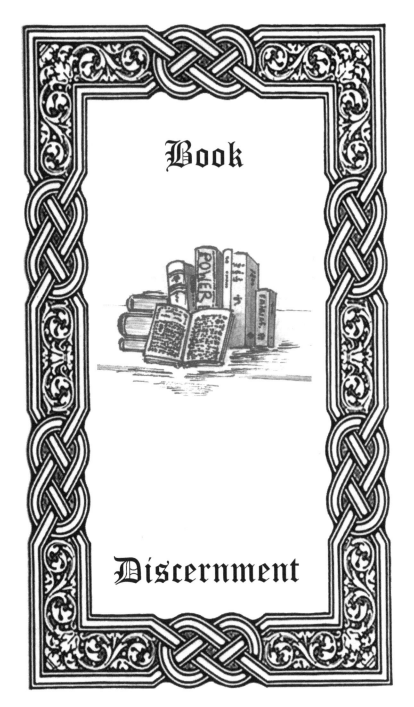

Discernment

96

'What Goes Around, Comes Around'

You have become fatigued with being knocked back, time after time and what you need to do right now is take a long hard look at what you are doing and where it is actually taking you, because it seems as though you are going nowhere fast. If you keep insisting on making the same mistakes then you will continue running round on this hamster wheel that, quite frankly, you have created for yourself. You need to make changes in how you think, and treat others. You are being given a 'wakeup call' to bring about the life you so desperately desire. It won't happen overnight and will take hard work on your part, but it will be worth it. Take a look at self-help books on topics such as positive thinking or cosmic ordering and you will realise that you are what you create. So go on, do yourself a favour and jump off this merry-go-round and live life!

Dowsing Revealed

Dowsing is a natural sensory perception used by birds, animals and man. It was depicted in cave drawings found in Spain dating back 50,000 years. In Tutankhamen's tomb dowsing tools were also found. King Henry VIII employed a treasure finder named George Dowser. Queen Elizabeth I had German dowsers come to England to teach dowsing to miners. Dowsing is known by many other names throughout the world, and was originally used to find water, food and shelter. Dowsers are sometimes called 'Water Witches'. **Dowsing reveals...** Don't be afraid to make changes. See through new eyes, with a new perspective. Let go of the old.

Dowsing

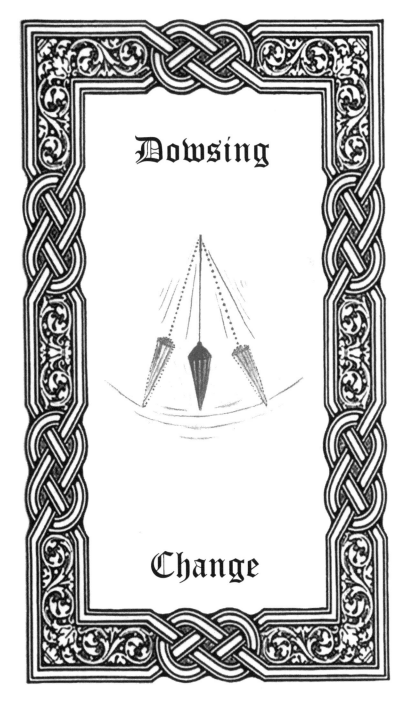

Change

97

'Variety is the Spice of Life'

Each day just seems to drag and you never get to achieve anything. This isn't how you envisaged your life. What happened? Who have you become? A person who has become stuck in their ways, that's who. How can you expect to have exciting experiences if you won't try something new? The less you do the less courage you will have to try. That may be all well and good for someone who has no desire to make something of their life. But that's not you. Your soul is crying out for some fun, some adventure. You are being urged to bite the bullet and just go for it. The more you experience, the stronger and more confident you will become. You will begin to enjoy being who you are as you work towards reaching your full potential. You couldn't do it if you didn't want to, but you can achieve each and every dream, because you do want to, don't you?

Charm Bracelet Revealed

The charm bracelet derives from Ancient Greece. The bracelet was endowed with magical powers by chanting an incantation over each individual piece that was gifted or collected from various places of significance. This became consecrated and then known as a 'lucky charm'. Charm bracelets were worn to signify important events in life and signified who a person was. They were used so that the Gods would recognise who they were when they passed over to the spirit world. **Charm Bracelet reveals...** Play more. Make a list of your goals and aspirations. Ask for guidance and take action. Don't play it safe. It is time to take a risk.

Charm Bracelet

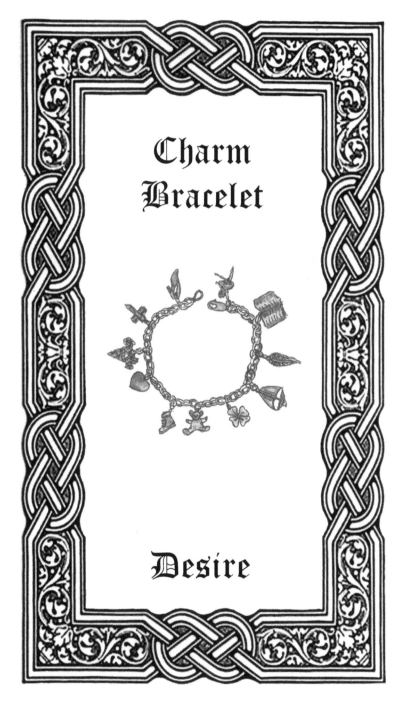

Desire

98

'Better Safe Than Sorry'

Caution! If you have been considering making a move then now is most definitely not the right time to do so. You are going through a period where it is more sensible to keep things as they are. It is preferable to be cautious at this time, rather than face any unpleasantness through rash actions. Any major decisions can also be put on hold. Do not throw caution to the wind, as you often do. Instead, think of this as a time of rest, of incubation, until you get another sign to move forward. You are also asked to put in measures to ensure your safety, such as switching off electrical plugs, regularly checking oil and water levels in your car, as well as tyre pressures and installing a smoke alarm. You are not in any danger, but need be in a place of awareness of what could happen, and take necessary steps of prevention. Once you have done so all will be well.

Lock Revealed

The oldest lock known to us was found by archaeologists in the Khorsabad Palace ruins near Nineveh. The lock was estimated to be 4,000 years old. Locks were used in Ancient Egypt around that time. The old gates of the city of Jerusalem had locks made of wood. The invention of the lock enabled imprisonment and also privacy. Women in history were forced to wear chastity belts, which were locked to prevent them from engaging in sexual activity. **Lock reveals...** Wait or look at different options. Ask for help. Be open to receiving assistance from another. Keep yourself to yourself whilst you regroup. Put into place protection for you and your family. Focus on your own needs at this time.

Lock

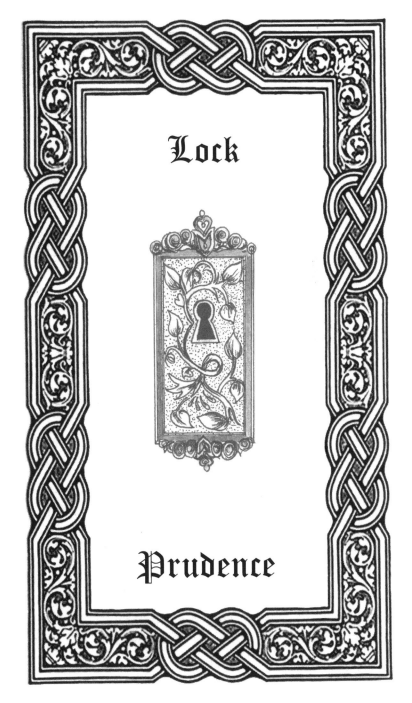

Prudence

99

'Out With the Old, In With the New'

Saddle up, it's time to gallop off into the sunset. Come on, even you must realise that you can't continue down this path. While you have been unable to move on, others have been running rings around you in order to get their way. You have allowed this to happen mainly out of a warped sense of duty. Changes need to be made and your feelings of obligation to others will be the first to go. Don't be afraid to be dramatic, allow others to see that you mean business. This is your life, and now is the moment to bring it in line with who you really are and how you would love it to be. Get rid of anything, or anyone, that could hold you back or bring you down. You can do this in a kind and loving way, but be assertive and put in your boundaries. This is your time to say 'No' to what no longer is needed in your life, and a big fat 'Yes!' to life itself.

Horseshoe Revealed

Horseshoes were hung outside houses to prevent malevolent faeries entering, as they are repelled by the dense energy of metal. The horseshoe is presented as a talisman in *The True Legend of St. Dunstan and the Devil* as a charm against witchcraft. Superstitious sailors believe nailing a horseshoe to the mast will help avoid storms. Today a bride often carries a silk version with her bouquet for a fruitful marriage. **Horseshoe reveals...** Don't commit yourself. Learn to say 'No' to others requests and demands. Be more assertive. Release feelings of guilt. Don't do anything out of obligation. Stop trying to be a people pleaser. Start putting yourself first. Know that you are worthy. Treat yourself with respect. Live life for yourself.

Horseshoe

Replenish

100

'Mighty Oaks From Little Acorns Grow'

Keep going! It may seem unlikely to you at the moment, but everything will work out perfectly. You just need to know how to nurture your ideas. Like a gardener your thoughts are like seeds and need to be fed and watered with positive expectations. Patience can be the biggest challenge for you. Know that even though you may not see the seeds mature, they are growing nonetheless. This is when all the magic happens as the universe works hard, putting together all that is needed to develop the dream that you planted. As the shoots begin to show, take action by putting into place your plans. Belief is the key ingredient. Success awaits you. It may take a little time, but it's worth it. All good things come to those who wait and remember that great things come from small beginnings.

Acorn Revealed

To the Druids, the oak was a gateway to other realms. Carrying or wearing a necklace of acorns was believed to provide protection and shelter when passing to the spirit world. Norse legend tells of Thor sheltering from a thunderstorm under a mighty oak tree. Acorns were left on windowsills to protect the house from a lightning strike. The acorn is a good luck symbol representing spiritual growth, strength and power. To carry an acorn prevents loneliness, illness and pain. If gathered on a full moon, acorns make a good Faery talisman, which brings luck and prosperity. **Acorn reveals...** You have a great idea, run with it. Don't discount ideas for fear of others' ridicule. Your career or business will prosper. Enjoy the process. Make a financial investment.

Acorn

Maturity

101

'A Picture Paints a Thousand Words'

You have recently witnessed, or are about to witness, something that shocks you. You will not want to believe it and will be open to all the verbal excuses under the Sun because you don't want it to be true. But your eyes are not the deceivers. No matter what is said please know that what you have seen is as clear as day. This message also comes to warn you to consider how you come across to others. It is time to take inventory of your behaviour and appearance. Where it is great to be individual and a free spirit, it is important to hold yourself in high regard too. Have respect for yourself. You will find that reactions from those around you will be entirely different to what you are used to and you will feel more valued. Remember your actions create pictures in people's minds, so think carefully about the way in which you would like to illustrate the story of your life.

Window Revealed

The earliest windows were just holes in the wall. The Romans were the first to use glass for windows. In 1696 a window tax was introduced in England and similar taxes lasted until the 19th century in parts of Europe, hence the saying 'daylight robbery'. A window symbolises freedom and passage. The eyes are called 'the windows to the soul'. **Window reveals...** Your spiritual sight is opening. Trust your visions. Take care over your appearance. Know that you are worthy. Don't judge someone new on their looks. Remember that everything you imagine is seen in the spirit world. See through new eyes, with a new perspective. Try to see a situation through the eyes of the other person. Look at the world through the eyes of love.

Window

Perspective

102

'If You Can't Stand the Heat...'

Enough is enough! You want to throw in the towel, but feel that by doing so you dessert your commitments and responsibilities. Perhaps you should persevere as it might get better. This message comes to assure you that actually it won't improve. You are being advised to get out! If you can't handle the pressure then leave it to someone who can. Don't look upon this as a sign of failure. You have done nothing wrong. You are just being asked to recognise your strengths and weaknesses. Find something else that fulfils you. The moment you walk away you will feel so much better and will be freed to achieve your full potential elsewhere. It is always commendable to try to reach for the main course, but so silly to allow ourselves to drown in the soup. So take the pressure off and go find something that rightly matches your talents and interests.

Cauldron Revealed

Cauldrons have been used since then Bronze Age as cooking vessels. The cauldron is one of the four treasures of the Tuatha De Danaan, known to supply food endlessly, so no one would ever go hungry. It was called the Cauldron of the Dagda. Cauldrons are linked to the Welsh Goddess Cerridwen and represent the womb; a place of spiritual and physical alchemy, the sacred space that allows for creation to take place and the home of great wisdoms. **Cauldron reveals...** You are on the wrong path. Look to see what truly fuels your passion. Don't worry about letting anyone else down. Take steps towards following your life's purpose.

Cauldron

Superfluous

103

'On Cloud Nine'

Oh happy days! You are in a state of bliss and couldn't be happier. It took a while for everything to work out but now it has and you are reaping the rewards. Often this happens when we totally let go, without forcing anything. For instance, if someone has fallen in love with another who is not as interested, then the key is to release the energy of desperation and stand back. This allows the universe to weave its magic, and the union is created and comes together when least expected. Wonderful, when you know how, isn't it? The feeling of elation that you are experiencing now is also contributing to your self-confidence and wellbeing. You are free from worrying and have finally found peace of mind. This is what it is all about. The state of Nirvana is where so many people aspire to be, and you have reached it. Congratulations!

Cloud Revealed

More than 2,000 years ago clouds were honoured and believed to contain very mystical qualities as well as being used to divine the weather and thereby govern the cycles of food production. The Druids were, and still are, known for cloud busting, which is an old technique to move clouds, so that the rain would not fall, or they would not cast a shadow. The Celts also practised cloud divination to predict the weather and read various meanings from their shapes. In Greek mythology the clouds were the daughters of Oceanus, having been drawn up to the heavens. **Cloud reveals...** Success is yours. Your dreams have come into fruition, or will do very soon. Rest assured that victory is yours. Don't change a thing.

Cloud

Euphoria

104

'Don't Look Back'

The only way is up! Yes, you may have felt hurt or betrayed; however, the only way forward is to take the lesson on board so that you are not knocked for six, should you be in the same situation again. Because your perception will have changed you can create a more harmonious life, especially in the face of adversity. We can choose to see all situations as amazing lessons, whether easy or hard. By doing this you will be filled with wonderful gifts of gratitude. This is when you become the observer, watching the drama act out and even though you may appear to be taking part, you are no longer affected by the lines or the actions. Soon nothing will faze you and all that you attract into your life will be more harmonious and peaceful. So no more playing the victim, take the role of the wise and learned one instead, which you will become naturally as you grow.

Mushroom Revealed

The Aztecs and the Egyptian Pharaohs considered this edible fungus to be the food of the Gods. Circles of mushrooms found in woods and fields alike are called fairy rings. These are believed to be portals the fairies use to enter from their realm into this world and get back again. The magic mushroom induces an altered state of mind when consumed. Aristotle and Plato participated in religious ceremonies at Eleusis, known as the Eleusian Mysteries. It is said that the rituals involved taking mind-altering substances such as magic mushrooms. **Mushroom reveals...** A bright future awaits you. You are provided for in all ways. Hold a positive outcome in your thoughts. This is a time of growth.

Mushroom

Expansion

105

'No News is Good News'

Have patience! It seems as though you have been waiting an age to receive news. It won't come any quicker no matter how much fretting you do. It is, of course, understandable that you are anxious as it seems that what you would love to happen hasn't actually come to fruition yet. But worry not, as it will. You just need to trust! It is important to know that you have put in place all the necessary steps in order for what you want to happen, to come about. But you must allow everything to unfold naturally. Things that you cannot see need to take place, in the background, to bring it about. So, even though you may be chomping at the bit, you are required to have a little faith and trust that everything is in divine order. Feel the anticipation, but in an excited way, knowing that you really will get the results you are hoping for. The biggest surprise is when!

Letter Revealed

Letters have existed since the times of Ancient Egypt, Rome, China, India, Sumer and Greece. Letters made up several of the books of the Bible. Back in the Dark Ages and for centuries afterwards letters were sealed with hot candle wax and often a family crest was imprinted into this. Riders carried news, through letters, on horseback, to deliver up and down countries. Henry VIII established a Master of the Post in 1516, which was the birth of England's Royal Mail delivery service. **Letter reveals...** Trust that all is well. Your dreams are happening, just have patience. You will receive news from an unexpected source.

Letter

Trust

106

'Put Your Best Foot Forward'

A new way of thinking will help you to embrace life. Spruce yourself up, in appearance if you will, but definitely in mind. Embark on a task, or journey, with a new and positive attitude. In Walt Disney's movie, Mary Poppins, the nanny tells the children that they are going to play a game called 'Tidying up the Nursery'. The little boy, Michael, replies, 'That doesn't sound like much of a game.' Mary replies that it all depends on how they look at it. Well, in the end they have great fun. Everything can be magical, enjoyable even, if done with gusto and purpose. As you face anything in this way you will find that you achieve much more than you ever have. People's attitudes towards you will positively change, as yours will to others. When we change ourselves, so too does the world directly around us. So, come on put a little effort in and go for it. A whole new way of life is waiting.

Foot Revealed

The complementary healing art of reflexology, based on the same energetic principles as acupuncture, has been documented in Ancient China, India and Egypt. Pictures were discovered of reflexology being performed on Buddha and in Egyptian tombs. In India, 5,000 years ago, the feet were thought to symbolise the unity of the entire universe. The sole of the foot was considered sacred and it was believed that when a foot treads on the land it is taking ownership of the Earth. **Foot reveals...** Don't give up. You are stronger than you realise. Put your focus into your heart's desire. See yourself in the best light possible. Avoid judgement.

Foot

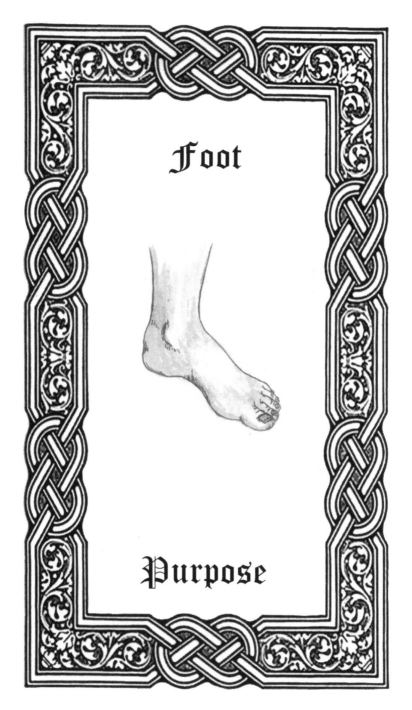

Purpose

107

'Be Careful What You Wish For'

There is something that you desire so strongly that nothing else matters. All your dreams will come true and you will live happily ever after – really? Your obsession for a possession has blinded you to unseen factors that could accompany the attainment of your desire. In the Wiccan tradition a verbal request to Spirit always ends with the saying, 'With harm to none'. Realise that suffering could occur as a result of your wish being granted. A person may wish for money and this may result in them ending up in a nasty accident and receiving the money in compensation. Seeking fame could result in a person's private life being sprawled across the papers – achieving fame, but not necessarily how they hoped. You must be clear about what you wish for. When you realise this and live accordingly you might find you no longer require what you once desired.

Aladdin's Lamp Revealed

Aladdin's Lamp is a popular tale in the Middle Eastern The Arabian Nights stories. When the lamp is rubbed a powerful genie appears and grants the master of the lamp three wishes. Throughout the ages people have been consumed with greed and an easy route to access treasures. The lamp is the epitome of this. The genie symbolises the teacher who though able to grant any wish is also mindful of the lessons within. The act of rubbing a lamp is not always the most fruitful way to quench our desires, especially if we have not thought about what these gains really mean. **Aladdin's Lamp reveals...** Be mindful of your wishes, words and thoughts.

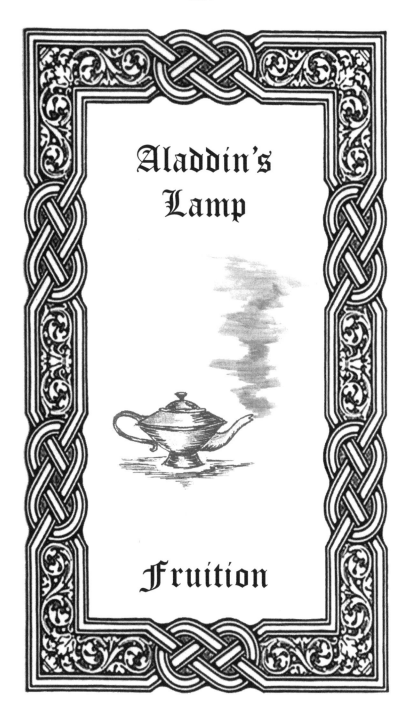

Aladdin's Lamp

Fruition

108

'You've Hit the Nail on the Head'

It has taken a while for the penny to drop, but at last you have listened to your intuition. An 'Aha!' moment has hit you and it's as though you have awoken from a deep slumber and seen the light. The message has come to you to confirm that you are right. There may be others who claim otherwise, but you are being urged to stick to your guns here. Others will come around in time, and even if they don't, you can move forward knowing that you are correct. Isn't it wonderful when something that has been hidden is realised? A new gateway has now opened and you are able to step through it, into a world that will now seem to be quite different to how you had previously seen it. Being gifted with this fresh information will allow you to be more aware and discerning. Trust your intuition, and follow it accordingly, for it is absolutely bang on!

Gate Revealed

The Ishtar Gate, constructed in 575BC, made the initial list of the Seven Wonders of the Ancient World. The Pearly Gates of Heaven are said to be guarded by St Peter. In whatever guise, gates symbolise the entrance to further enlightenment; portals to other places, whether good or bad. They can be seen as the last obstacle or final hurdle to overcome in order to reach a place of realisation, seeing the truth for what it is which may even be scandalous. On these occasions scandals are often tagged as 'gates', 'Watergate' being perhaps the best known example. **Gate reveals...** You are correct. Be brave and take steps towards your dreams. Trust your intuition.

Gate

Realisation

109

'Don't Teach Your Grandma to Suck Eggs'

You like to get the job done and for it to be done well, but it is time to let go of controlling everything. If you just step back and observe other people you will realise that everyone has their strengths and experiences to bring to the table. When you insist on advising those who have more experience then you are just being annoying. Do you really want this to be people's opinion of you? You may not like the words in this message, but do yourself a favour and take heed. Only the strong can look within and admit that changes need to be made. Why do you disallow yourself to confess that you might not know something? It isn't a weakness to admit to these things. So try to step back and realise that though you may know a fair bit, there are actually others who know a lot more and by doing so you will truly benefit from others' wisdom.

Pandora's Box Revealed

Pandora's Box was in fact a jar, an artefact in Greek mythology, that was given to the first woman, Pandora, on Earth as a gift by the God Zeus. Under strict instructions not to open it, she nevertheless lifted the lid and it let out all manners of evil into the world. It is a story to explain how the ills of the world began. An epic poem about Pandora's Box, called Theogeny, was written by Hesiod in 800BC. To open a 'Pandora's Box' means opening up something that could lead to dire consequences. **Pandora's Box reveals...** Admit your true feelings. Develop your sensitivity. Be empathetic. Take advice. Seek another's opinion. Be willing to listen and learn.

Pandora's Box

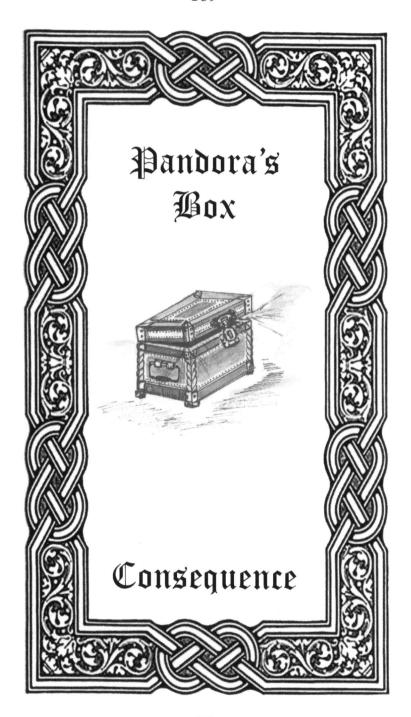

Consequence

110

'You're on a Wild Goose Chase'

Whatever is running wild in your imagination, it is time for a reality check! Nothing wrong with dreams and aspirations, but there comes a point when it is time to face up to the fact that it just ain't gonna happen! You seriously can't expect all that you want to just fall into your lap. A little effort at least must be put in. Please do not believe every promise that is made to you. Things are not all that they seem and you need to become aware that there are underlying reasons for this person to act as though they have your best interests at heart. You are not heading in the right direction. Do not go any further, for you must seek an alternative route. If you choose to start again then please try to be less skittish and more discerning. Stand strong; learn from this experience and you shan't come down to Earth without such a big bump after all.

Feather Revealed

Falling feathers are looked upon as a sign from deceased loved ones. White feathers indicate angelic communion. Feathers have been revered since Stone Age times. They are used in arrows to help with flight. In Victorian times a coward was presented with white feathers. The Prince of Wales has a signet with three feathers on it. Native American tribes adorned their hair and body with feathers. Each headdress worn varied from tribe to tribe and feathers were earned through bravery and initiation. In their tradition feathers are also used for cleansing, smudging and to pray with. **Feather reveals...** Be cautious. Ground and centre yourself. Take sensible steps towards your dreams, not short cuts. Ask the angels for help.

Feather

Flight

111

'It is Written in the Stars'

You have an important life purpose and it is time to get on with it. You feel special and know that you are meant to be 'big'. But even though you have felt a calling, you don't know what it is you are meant to do. We choose the exact time of our birth and astrological signs, stars and planetary movement all participate in this choice. Astrology influences your very being, the lessons to be learnt, and strengths to enable you to do what you must. For example if you chose to be born at 1am on October 9, the month dictates you are under the star sign of Libra, thus bringing the focus of balance and fairness into your life. The number 9 represents life purpose and completion. There are many other factors too such as rising signs, moons and planets associated with our birth. We come from the stars, and so by looking at our chart we are shown what could be in store for us. Yes, we create our own destiny but the stars point us in the right direction. Seek out an accredited astrologer and get your astrological chart read. A lot of answers will be revealed to you.

Astrology Revealed

The Ancient Babylonians birthed astrology, introducing it to the Greeks in 4th Century BC. Plato and Aristotle ensured astrology became highly regarded as a science, with its most common logo now being the Zodiac. 'Zodiac' means a circle of animals. The world's first Zodiac horoscope was created in Dendera, Egypt. **Astrology reveals...** The answers you seek will be revealed. Study numerology. You have an important life purpose to make the world a better place. Time to shine your light. Happiness awaits.

Astrology

Destiny

About The Authors

Barbara Meiklejohn-Free is the UK's best loved and hardest working 'Wisdom Keeper' – teacher, advocate and protector of the great Earth-centred traditions. She has been working with Spirit since the age of twelve. She takes mediumship, psychic abilities, shamanic healing, rebirthing, soul retrieval, past life regression and rites of passage, combining them all together in her readings and raising them to new levels of awareness in order to help people become aware of who they are and why they are here. Best-selling author Barbara also leads people on guided site visits across the globe to meet the native people, to gain an understanding first-hand of the way they live according to the teachings of Mother Earth. She worked at the Arthur Findlay College as a course organiser and workshop leader and teaches at the College of Psychic Studies in London.

www.facebook.com/barbara.meiklejohnfree.5
www.spiritvisions.co.uk
You Tube – Barbara Meiklejohn-Free

Flavia Kate Peters is an author, speaker, therapist, singer and a natural mystic who connects with the ancient deities of the Celtic British Isles. Known as 'The Faery Shaman', Flavia Kate works very closely with the nature spirits and faeries. As a child Flavia Kate often heard the angels singing and connected with their messages effortlessly, as she still does. She offers readings and guidance as well as giving talks and workshops at events and shows throughout the year. She is a Reiki and Crystal Master, Angel Therapist® and a spiritual counsellor. Flavia Kate is a regular columnist for FAE Magazine and teaches her popular Angel Energy Practitioner® certification programme worldwide.

www.facebook.com/flaviakate
www.flaviakatepeters.com

MOON
BOOKS

Moon Books invites you to begin or deepen your encounter with
Paganism, in all its rich, creative, flourishing forms.